GOVERNMENT WORKS

GOVERNMENT WORKS

Why Americans Need the Feds

MILTON J. ESMAN

CORNELL UNIVERSITY PRESS

ITHACA AND LONDON

First published 2000 by Cornell University Press

Printed in the United States of America

Library of Congress Cataloging-in-Publication Data

Esman, Milton J. (Milton Jacob), 1918–
    Government works : why Americans need the Feds / Milton J. Esman.
      p. cm.
    Includes bibliographical references and index.
    ISBN 0-8014-3759-9
    1. Political planning—United States.   2. United States—Politics and
government—1993–   3. Conservatism—United States.   I. Title.

JK468.P64 E75 2000
320.52′0973—dc21

                                          99-059992

Cloth printing   10 9 8 7 6 5 4 3 2 1

FSC FSC Trademark © 1996 Forest Stewardship Council A.C.
SW-COC-098

CONTENTS

PREFACE

The dominant theme of right-wing politics and public discourse during the past quarter century has been an unrelenting campaign to demonize government, chiefly the federal government, and to shrink its size and influence in American society and the American economy. This campaign has been waged, successfully, by ideological zealots and Republican politicians and financed by corporate interests bent on maximizing their freedom of action by reducing government regulations and minimizing their tax obligations. Hostility to government has become the rhetorical mantra and the defining core of modern American conservatism.

The response from progressive writers and commentators, and from Democratic politicians, has been so hesitant, so compromising, and so void of passion that in the absence of effective opposition, conservatives have seized the intellectual initiative and assumed control of the public agenda. This anti-government bias runs contrary to the main thrust of American political and economic experience and is detrimental to the well-being of the American nation on the brink of the new millennium.

This brief book examines this central predicament in public affairs and proposes a rationale, a set of policies, and a political strategy for restoring necessary balance to public discourse and political action. It is addressed especially to those who, like the author, have been troubled by the unchallenged trashing of a central institution of American democracy.

I am grateful to Jerome Ziegler, Theodore Lowi, and Leonard Weinstein for their astute and helpful comments on an earlier version of this book, and to James Harney and Marwan Hanania for valuable research assistance.

MILTON J. ESMAN

Ithaca, New York

GOVERNMENT WORKS

CHAPTER ONE

Is Government the Problem?

Government is not the solution to our problem, government is the problem.

—Ronald Reagan, Inaugural Address, January 20, 1981

During the final quarter of the twentieth century the most significant mood in American public affairs has been disenchantment with government. This mood has ranged from cynicism to militant hostility, bordering in some instances on hysteria and criminal violence, as in the Oklahoma City bombing. In response to a question posed by the Gallup organization, "Do you trust your government to do the right thing all of the time or most of the time," in 1963, 75 percent responded affirmatively.[1] A generation later, in 1995, only 20 percent agreed.[2] In a 1999 survey, 68 percent of the 18–34 age cohort felt "disconnected from government."[3] This collapse of confidence in government, especially among the nation's youth, is momentous in view of the problems faced by the United States and all post-industrial societies. It is, moreover, a dramatic example of American exceptionalism. A recent survey of beliefs in government in Western European democracies shows "little change over time and scant evidence of a mood swing in favor of rolling back the state, even in those countries where the welfare state is most developed."[4] What accounts for this sharp reaction against government in the American mind-set, what are the implications of the prevailing alienation from public authority for the health and well-being of American society, and is this mood likely to be sustained indefinitely?

1

The Indictment of Government

The assault on government as a negative, even insidious force in American life was the main theme of the 1994 Republican political sweep and of their 1996 national campaign. The apostles of this doctrine, the New Right, had scored their first success with Ronald Reagan's stunning triumph in 1980. They had taken control of the Republican Party, reshaped it as their political instrument, determined to roll back Roosevelt's New Deal, Johnson's Great Society, the civil rights, women's lib, environmentalist and consumer protection movements, and sought to impress their doctrine of minimal government, traditional morality, and laissez-faire economics on the nation's social, economic, and cultural policies. Though they suspect government at all levels, the main target has been the federal government. Their allergy to active government has become the dominant theme in American public discourse.

Though important interest groups in American society have militantly supported this crusade against government, it is driven, like no movement in American history since Prohibition early in this century, by ideology. The thematic components of this campaign against government have been reiterated with such persistence and such vehemence that they have achieved the status of conventional wisdom. Government, the New Right insists, is inherently coercive and threatening to individual liberty; self-serving legislators, the willing tools of "special interests," and meddlesome, power-hungry bureaucrats are engaged in a criminal conspiracy to encroach on the rights of ordinary citizens, for example, threatening property rights by intrusive environmental regulations, violating Second Amendment rights by gun control measures, jeopardizing the livelihoods of small businessmen by product safety rules, affirmative action requirements, and onerous occupational safety regulations which serve no public purpose but pander to special interests and bureaucratic aggrandizement. Confiscatory taxes and meddlesome regulations, they assert, have undermined American economic competitiveness.

Government, the indictment continues, is congenitally incompetent, wasteful, and inefficient. It imposes onerous burdens on hard-pressed taxpayers, consumes tax revenues in unproductive bureaucracy, and dissipates them on unworthy parasites, notably "welfare" that benefits unwed women who choose to have numerous illegitimate offspring so that they can avoid honest work while continuing to thrive on government handouts. Tax-and-spend government, moreover, does nothing right; it is the chronic victim of the "law" of unintended consequences. Year after year, it "throws money" after problems such as drug abuse, teenage pregnancy, and inner-city poverty with no assurance that any of them will work, and persists with them long after they have demonstrably failed. Politicians and bureaucrats lack the accountability and the competitive profit incentive that produce both effectiveness and efficiency in private enterprise. Despite good intentions, government makes many of these problems even worse. It is simply not the appropriate vehicle for tackling the nation's social and economic problems. Thus the principal motif in the Republicans' successful attack on President Clinton's ill-fated proposals for restructuring health care in 1993 was that they would commit the nation's health services to an army of incompetent, intrusive, power-hungry and wasteful federal government bureaucrats.

Government, according to the New Right, is inherently vulnerable to corruption. The more taxpayers' dollars they have to play with, the greater the temptation for politicians. The most lurid recent evidences in support of this image have been the Whitewater allegations, the 1996 campaign finance scandals, and highly publicized instances of fraud and abuse by prominent congressmen, including former Democratic Speaker Jim Wright and former Republican Speaker Newt Gingrich.

But the overarching charge is that the federal government has been captured by a "liberal counter-cultural establishment," elitist, non-representative, serving such aggressive special interests as homosexuals, abortionists, gun control advocates, labor unions, African Americans and other minorities, women's liberationists, and godless "secular humanists"—none of them representative of the mainstream of God-fearing, hard-working, law-abiding, taxpaying American citizens.[5] The federal government must first be redeemed from this liberal establishment by a political and cultural revolution and restored to the people. Even during the twelve-year era of conservative Republican presidents Reagan and Bush, the "liberals," they believed, continued to rule Washington by their domination of Congress and the federal bureaucracy and their control of universities, major foundations, the mass media, and the federal judiciary. The federal courts have been complicit in the unconstitutional expansion of government power by reading their own liberal preferences into the Constitution. To reverse this trend,

Presidents Reagan and Bush were careful to appoint only what they considered to be judicial "conservatives" to the federal bench.

By an unrelenting intellectual crusade against these false, shallow, exotic, and immoral ideas, the liberal establishment could be discredited, dethroned, and replaced by a new establishment grounded in authentic American morality and experience. The cultural revolution would be implemented by restricting abortions, limiting homosexuals' rights, promoting school prayer, banning pornography on TV and other mass media, and federal financing of private, including religiously sponsored, schools by educational vouchers. The solution to the evils of big govenment is to cut back and strictly limit its interference in social and economic affairs by deregulation, marketization, privatization, devolution of services to the states, and strict interpretation of the Constitution by the courts. Then by rigorously circumscribing its taxing and regulatory powers, the federal government could once again be limited to its essential functions.

Among these essential functions are national defense and law enforcement. The Republican right has been unfailingly solicitous of the armed forces, excluding them from attacks on bureaucratic wastefulness and incompetence. They favor generous financing, including a second round of Star Wars. While they advocate more severe penalties for criminals, the construction of additional prisons, and expanded use of capital punishment, they oppose federal expenditures for crime prevention. But though the logic of their case for minimal government and enhanced individual responsibility would have called for the elimination or privatization of Social Security (old age and survivors' insurance) as proposed three decades ago by Senator Goldwater, and the privatization as well of Medicare, Republicans are careful to avoid directly attacking these large, popular middle-class entitlement programs.

The New Right's hostility to the federal government and to the nation's poor has been accompanied by a nativist suspicion and distrust of the motives of foreigners, thus to any form of international cooperation, especially with the United Nations. While their influential corporate constituency has compelled them to acquiesce in free trade initiatives, their disdain for foreigners has been directed at the hapless and defenseless United Nations. Republican-controlled Congresses have allowed unpaid financial obligations to the UN to exceed $1.6 billion.[6] After compelling the UN to adopt numerous administrative reforms and to downsize its staff, on the implicit understanding that their adoption would result in the release of the laggard U.S. payments, Congress in 1997 defaulted on these payments. Similar obligations to the IMF and the World Bank remain unpaid. Clinging to an isolationist "Fortress America" definition of America's national interests and responsibilities, the Republican congressional leadership condemned U.S. participation in the NATO campaign to restrain ethnic cleansing in Kosovo, dubbing it "Clinton's War."

The attack on big government has been militantly, even angrily, ideological in tone, as illustrated by the pitbull debating tactics of the former Republican leader and principal party strategist Newt Gingrich. The massive fiscal deficits and expansion in the national debt, from $914 billion in 1980 to $4.4 trillion in 1993, had occurred under Republican presidents who sharply reduced revenues while increasing military expenditures.[7] Though Republicans to a man voted against President Clinton's 1993 deficit reduction package—because it restored modest progressivity to the federal income-tax schedules and raised rates on wealthier taxpayers—in 1994 they succeeded in blaming the deficits on "tax and spend" liberal Democrats. They pledged to eliminate deficits by a balanced budget amendment to the Constitution and, in late 1995, unveiled a package of drastic cutbacks that would produce a balanced budget in seven years, featuring reductions in federal contributions to welfare, Medicare, Medicaid (health service to the poor), and student education loans. Though they overextended themselves and suffered a serious setback in public esteem when they closed the federal government in late 1995, their basic strategy has not changed. The unexpected emergence of fiscal surpluses during Clinton's second term has, however, undermined the credibility of attacks on Democrats as tax-and-spend liberals.

Rightist Strategies and the Progressive Response

By constant repetition of these themes, beginning in the early 1980s, the Republican right gradually gained the ideological initiative. They were assisted, unwittingly, by large segments of middle-class youth who had little sympathy for their social and economic objectives but were alienated from politics and government and from all forms of authority (the "establishment") by the rebellious youth culture of the

1960s and the experience of the Vietnam War. The Republican right had a simple set of explanations for the country's ills, and these explanations resonated with an increasingly insecure and angry electorate that for nearly a generation had been losing confidence in government. The Vietnam War, Watergate, the double-digit inflation of the late 1970s, the Iran hostage debacle, Irangate, stagnation in real family incomes, the corrosive threat of violent crime to personal security, corruption in high places—these created a mood that provided political space for apostles of minimal government and lower taxes who were prepared to focus blame on government for these many failings and grievances. The failure of Democratic politicians and spokespersons of the moderate left to respond to these discontents allowed the Republican right to redefine the agenda of American politics without effective challenge. By 1994, despite Democratic control of the presidency and the Congress, intellectually the moderate left was bankrupt. Elected Democratic politicians, including a Democratic president, were reduced to coopting Republican themes—lower taxes, less regulation, balanced budgets, reduced welfare payments, devolution to the states—or appealing to separate constituencies in the language of the 1960s to sustain particular programs such as Social Security, Medicare, civil rights, and environmental protection. Republicans successfully converted a belated public concern with fiscal deficits plus a growing hostility to taxes, welfare, and crime into a political crusade to limit, then permanently disable, the federal government.

Spokespersons for the right have persuaded themselves that the most effective case they can muster to discredit and defeat a measure they oppose is to argue that it would increase the scope of the federal government and the role of bureaucrats. The merits of the proposal seem almost incidental. This strategy has been pursued by the tobacco companies in their saturation advertising campaign to defeat proposals to regulate cigarette ads addressed to teenagers and to compensate the victims of nicotine addiction and the state governments that have borne many of the costs of their medical care; by insurance companies and health maintenance organizations (HMOs) to block the proposed "patients' bill of rights" that would regulate abuses by HMOs and permit aggrieved patients to sue for damages in the courts; by the Republican congressional leadership determined to prevent expanded federal provisions of child care for working mothers, or increased federal aid for improved teacher training and repairs to dilapidated school buildings. So successful has been the rightist campaign to discredit the federal government that this has become the strategy of choice for powerful interest groups and their political allies who believe it can influence public opinion decisively. Next only to cutting taxes, the anti-government theme has become the most reliable standby of rightist politicians and candidates.

The collapse of the Soviet Union in 1991 confirmed the rightist conviction that associates active government with political tyranny and economic incompetence. Liberalism implies socialism, socialism implies communism, and liberals during the post–World War II period had been allegedly "soft" on communism. The godless Soviet experiment with big government, economic planning, and the welfare state had manifestly failed; at enormous human cost it impoverished whole societies, exactly as rightist spokesmen had predicted. For the United States and the rest of the world, the lessons were obvious: economic prosperity and well-being depend on free enterprise and market processes; to protect liberty and human rights, government must be curbed, and its activities limited to the essentials.

During this period there has been no principled defense or statement of the the need for or the benefits provided by an active federal government from any senior spokesperson for the Democrats or moderate left, including President Clinton. In fact, many have joined the populist chorus that disparages active government; President Clinton felt constrained to announce in his 1996 State of the Union message that "the era of big government is over."[8] So Democrats propose tax reductions, less in magnitude than those of the Republicans and focused, unlike the Republicans, more on the middle class than on wealthy taxpayers. They take their turn, along with their opponents, at bashing bureaucrats, and "reinventing" government, a trendy code word for reducing the size of the civil service, converting government employees to entrepreneurs, privatizing some functions, eliminating others, and devolving programs to the states. Implicitly, they accept much of the Republican-rightist diagnosis that the federal government has become too large, overextended, intrusive, overloaded, and out of control, as well as the rightist prescription that, where possible, market processes should supplant government administration. Yet, population increased between 1960 to 1995 by 47 percent, federal civilian employment grew by only 19 percent, and the federal civilian payroll decreased from 2.6 percent of GNP to 1.5.

That some federal agencies and programs should have been cut back or terminated in defiance of the interest groups that vigilantly protect them, that some regulations are indeed ineffective and intrusive, that new information-based technologies could provide better service to the public at less cost—these general propositions are not debatable. Administrative reform and the simplification of regulatory regimes must be an ongoing function of Congress and the Executive Branch. But Democratic politicians went much further in accepting the Republican indictment of government as though this had become an irrefutable premise for public policy. This behavior seems to be motivated by a need to compete with the Republican right in catering to what they believe to be the prevailing public mood—that government has become a burden rather than a benefit, a mood created in the first place by a steady, decades-long barrage of propaganda from Republican-rightist sources.

Progressively inclined intellectuals have been of little help.[9] As the welfare state became discredited by the image of wasteful spending, moral delinquency, and crime associated with overgenerous tax-funded "welfare" payments, and by charges of reverse discrimination attributed to affirmative action, progressives provided neither a convincing defense of these measures nor an alternative set of policy prescriptions. Keynesian economics, the consensus macroeconomic prescription for the three prosperous post–World War II decades, became largely irrelevant. Reagan's massive deficits precluded countercyclical federal expenditures or any new initiatives on social policy. And the free, transnational mobility of capital constrains macroeconomic policy choices by the state, even in so large and powerful an economy as the United States. The new vision of high-tech globalism dominated by giant lean-and-mean multinational corporations would render national governments virtually superfluous for economic management. Competitive efficiency in global markets would be the test of survival for these leviathans and their managers, and government dare not stand in their way.

And while mainstream Republicans embraced this vision, with their rediscovery of classical economics, social Darwinian morality, traditional "values," and rugged individualism, progressives failed to come forth with an alternative humanistic vision that might be converted by Democratic politicians into a winning platform. In fact, many left-leaning intellectuals and publicists were diverted from economic issues to such causes as multiculturalism, environmentalism, homosexual rights, and gender equality that appealed to important constituencies but failed to speak to the daily concerns of most workers, consumers, parents, and voters. Pragmatism in support of the status quo seemed as unpersuasive and as irrelevant as the Republican defense of laissez-faire economics during the Great Depression of the 1930s. In this book I intend to present the elements of an alternative humanistic vision and demonstrate that its fulfillment requires a strong and active federal government.

The New Right has succeeded in converting its hostility to the federal government into a political movement with a coherent ideology, abundant financial support, dedicated cadres of zealous activists, and enthusiastic mass constituencies. The movement combines a few simple themes: (1) laissez-faire economics, global capitalism, and unregulated market processes; (2) low taxes, minimal government, and states' rights; (3) suspicion of foreigners expressed as militarized unilateralism in foreign relations and hostility to racial minorities and immigrants who are believed to threaten the white Christian foundations of American society; and (4) the restoration of traditional morality, including the criminalization of abortion, pornography, and homosexuality, along with support for school prayer, restoration of the death penalty, and glorification of the home-making role of women. The several strands of this coalition, despite tensions within their ranks, have selected the Republican Party as their common political vehicle. They have taken control of that party at all levels of government, marginalized what remains of its "moderate" faction, and invested heavily in reshaping it to their image, ideologically and organizationally.[10]

Neither Republicans nor Democrats have been willing to address some of the main frustrations that vex the voting public, nor to deal with the underlying dilemmas facing American society even in an era of relative prosperity. Among the problems that both parties evade are these: the gnawing sense, among working Americans, of personal and family insecurity concerning employment, as corporations "downsize" their white-collar and professional as well as their blue-collar staffs, move manufacturing operations overseas, and hire more and more of their workers as "temporaries";[11] uncertainties about family health care as employers cut back on coverage in the face of higher costs; the stagnation of real earnings despite increased corporate profits, ballooning executive salaries, and the stock market boom of the 1990s; the housing crisis for low-income families; the struggle of moderate-income families to afford college tuition for their children without incurring heavy debt; in sum, multiple threats to the American dream that each generation would share in the rising productivity of the economy and realistically aspire to a better life and greater security than their parents.

Both parties in recent years have accepted, with varying degrees of enthusiasm, the liberal market paradigm as the foundation of U.S. economic policy. Despite lingering skepticism in labor and environmental circles and among a fringe of right-wing populists, free trade has become a bipartisan article of faith in policy-making circles.[12] It benefits U.S. consumers by providing goods at lower prices and has helped to win foreign markets for the more competitive high-tech segments of U.S. industry. Free trade has, however, wreaked havoc on millions of manufacturing workers, their families, and the communities they support as employers have transferred operations overseas to take advantage of much lower taxes and labor costs. Manufacturing employment in the United States fell from 25 percent of the labor force in 1970 to 15 percent in 1995.[13] Displaced employees and their communities have received scant readjustment assistance from government. The fate of these displaced manufacturing workers and of the once-proud communities they supported has been one of the silent tragedies of the past quarter century. Inflation-adjusted family incomes during the prosperous years of the late 1990s barely regained their late-1970s levels and have been maintained at middle-class levels mainly by combining overtime work and the earnings of husbands and wives.

The growing inequity in the distribution of income, which has deteriorated significantly since the mid-1970s, has produced troublesome economic as well as moral problems. Income distribution in the United States is now more skewed than in any other industrialized country or at any time in recent U.S. history.[14] Violent crime and delinquency, which disturb middle-class voters, as well as chronic poverty and deteriorating neighborhoods, are directly affected by the reduction and elimination of government programs that redistribute income by providing services to low-income families and neighborhoods. Because neither party knows how to deal with these problems within the present framework of public policy, they are evaded.

Then there are the mostly "unfelt" but nonetheless real problems. The chronic structural trade deficit appears to resist all macroeconomic remedies. At a rate approaching $300 billion a year, 3 percent of GDP, Americans have been consuming more than they produce, while the difference is financed by foreign borrowing. This unhealthy situation is attributed by most economists to the chronic and historically low rate of savings in the United States, which inflates consumer demand. Others hold that a contributing factor has been the sharp decline in manufacturing during the Reagan period that stripped the American economy of the capacity to produce many goods, such as clothing, textile products, and consumer electronics, which the American public demands in massive quantities and must now be imported. Although congressional Democrats in 1997 blocked the authorization of "fast track" authority in trade negotiations, neither party has been willing to confront the causes of this chronic imbalance, which threatens to accelerate as depressed Asian economies, taking advantage of depreciated currencies, attempt to export their way out of their current financial impasse.

The strategy or, more accurately, the expedient on which Democrats have relied—with the conspicuous exception of the president's failed health care reform—is to recommend marginal improvements in individual government programs, such as minimum wage, student loans, and health care for vulnerable groups, combined with tactical acceptance of many items—tax cuts, balanced budgets, welfare reform, devolution to the states—in the Republican-right agenda. These tactics have stripped the Republican right of much of their appeal to moderate voters. Excesses in their opponent's rhetoric and tactics, the mean-spirited zealotry of the Republican congressional majority, and threats to the entitlements of the elderly, environmental protection, and student loans, contributed to President Clinton's re-election campaign in 1996 and to modest Democratic successes in the 1998 mid-term elections. Such successes, however, have not generated public enthusiasm, as demonstrated by the very low voter turnouts; they have not challenged or even engaged the anti-government ideology promulgated by the New Right. This anti-government message appeals to a historic, deep-seated skepticism about the federal government in American popular culture, a distrust of politicians, and an allergy to taxes. It has a special attraction to certain constituencies, including gun owners and small businesspersons. Scapegoating the poor resonates with lingering but still active racist sentiments among segments of American society, including but by no means limited to southern white males; and corporate America remains willing to contribute generously to the campaigns of politicians who promise lower taxes and less regulation.

The Republican-rightist program would restore social Darwinism to a respectable place in American public morality. Those who are successful in life's competitive struggle should be encouraged and rewarded by public policy; others need to learn to shift for themselves, as men and women must be held responsible for their own fate. In this moral order, self-directed rugged individualism is honored, supplanting social solidarity, societal inclusiveness, altruism, and compassion for the weak and the fallen; people generally receive from life what they deserve. African Americans, for example, are said to be less successful because they are intellectually handicapped in their genetic endowments.[15] There should be little concern or responsibility, certainly not by government, for the losers of this world. Help must come from their families or the compassion and charity of churches and neighbors. Such themes revert to the standard morality of early capitalism, that of the nineteenth century. There remains, however, an unresolved tension between the Christian (Protestant evangelical) right, an important grassroots component of the Republican-right voting coalition, and corporate elites, along with their neo-conservative intellectual allies who provide much of the funding and the ideology for the movement and its policies. The latter tend to be libertarian or agnostic on moral and cultural matters while favoring low taxes and minimal government.

Equally reminiscent of the nineteenth century is the theme of rightist populism that extols state governments as the peoples' authentic tribunes, whereas the federal government speaks for special interests, bureaucrats, and liberal countercultual elites. Though the United States has become an unprecedentedly integrated economy with rapid interstate mobility of capital, labor, and information, though its economic structures and its public information networks have become highly centralized, the states are presented as economically and socially distinctive and close to the everyday lives, needs, and sentiments of their residents whose first loyalty is to their state governments. In contrast, the federal government is considered a remote, coercive, even foreign imposition on society, one that limits innovation and responsiveness in state governments and imposes rigid standard regulations on the great diversity represented by the states. Survey data indicate that substantial majorities of respondents express greater confidence in their state governments than in Washington.[16]

This renewed version of states' rights has become part of the conventional wisdom of the 1990s. Though inclined to insist on the maintenance of federal standards, President Clinton joins the Republican chorus in this rightist refrain, which would devolve to state governments functions that for more than a half century have been undertaken by Washington. This devolution was incorporated into the Republican-sponsored welfare reforms that Clinton signed into law in 1996.[17] The funding remains federal, but through the mechanism of bloc grants, state governments have broad discretion in allocating the grants; federal standards continue to apply, but they are less rigorous than previously, and some can be waived at the request of state governments. The same critics who claim that an integrating global economy precludes economic management and economic regulation by the federal government argue that despite a much more integrated United States economy, fifty states are better equipped than the federal government to deal with social, economic, and environmental affairs.

In promoting devolution to the states, the Republican right know very well what they are doing. It is part of their strategy to limit the role of the federal government on economic, environmental, and social matters while encouraging the states to enforce the moral agenda of their evangelical faction. With reduced federal funding and free of federal standards, many of these devolved functions, especially social and environmental services and regulations, will be hobbled financially or even abandoned by many state and local governments. In drifting with this tide, the Democrats demonstrate the absence of any guiding ideology or strategy. The appropriate division of responsibilities between Washington and the fifty states is important enough to warrant extended treatment in chapter 5.

The Progressives' Response

At the heart of this contest is the critical question of what should be the appropriate role of government in American society on the eve of the twenty-first century. At present, the Republican right promulgates and reiterates their vision of what this relationship should be. But what should have resulted in a great national debate and in the activation of a vigorous countermovement has not occurred. With rare exceptions, the Democratic left, including the intellectuals who support them, have abandoned the contest; they have been reduced to defending particular programs, criticizing particular Republican initiatives, or buying into populist rightist themes.

The organized forces in American society that could be mobilized to reinvigorate a new progressive movement operate independently of one another. Labor, environmentalists, African Americans, Hispanics, women, and homosexuals work on the fringes of the Democratic Party but do not invest in it or join in endowing it with a common vision.[18] It is precisely such a vision of the kind of America they seek to build that the current generation of progressive sympathizers has failed to evoke, a vision that might activate the broad strata of latent supporters who are dissatisfied with current trends in public policy but find the Democratic message sterile. Such a vision, rooted in the traditions of American progressivism, would emphasize such themes as (1) job and family security, including guaranteed health insurance; meaningful job retraining, placement, and relocation provisions for discharged employees; maternity leave and reliable day care for working families; and the maintenance by macroeconomic measures and fiscal policies of a full-employment economy; (2) quality of life, including extended forms of environmental protection, preservation of scenic and recreational riches, cultivation of the creative and performing arts, and presentation of non-commercial information and entertainment on TV and the airwaves; (3) expanded civil rights and opportunities, including strict enforcement of non-discrimination in employment, education, and housing, and improved access to higher education; and (4) international cooperation as a component of the U.S. national interest. Together, these themes are more than sufficient to outmatch the Republican-rightist vision that animates their movement and has prospered for more than two decades in the absence of a serious challenge.

To clarify these issues and to lay the groundwork for the debate that is so urgently needed, I consider it necessary first, to trace the combinations of interests, ideas, cultural attitudes, and beliefs that have affected these conflicts (chapter 2); to explore the evolution of positions taken on the role of government in the course of American history, beginning with the founding of the Republic (chapter 3); then to analyze and evaluate the merits of the current controversies in the context of the contemporary American economy, society, polity, and world role and to specify essential tasks that can be undertaken only by the federal government (chapters 4 and 5). Chapter 6 outlines the steps required to improve the operations of the federal government. Chapter 7 identifies component themes that respond to emergent needs, reflecting the principles that have guided our national development for two centuries. Chapter 8 outlines a winning political strategy for contemporary progressives.

Those who have read to this point will surely have detected that I am not neutral in this debate. I believe firmly that despite important lapses, the federal government has been, can be, and must continue to serve as a beneficent force in American society. In the absence of "energetic" federal action (Alexander Hamilton's term in *Federalist* No. 23), we cannot survive as a healthy society. I agree that the federal government should assume only those functions that cannot be better undertaken by individuals acting alone, by other associations, institutions, or public authorities. Despite rightist rhetoric to the contrary, this criterion has been followed throughout most of our history, including the New Deal of the 1930s and the Great Society of the 1960s. The presumption should be that the federal government is a resource available to the American people to meet needs that enhance their security, productivity, and quality of life. The federal state is indeed capable of such dangerous abuses of power as the alien and sedition laws of the 1790s, the internment of Japanese-American citizens during World War II, and the McCarthy era of the 1950s, but our pluralistic structures of government provide the means, as demonstrated in the Watergate crisis, for preventing, controlling, and rectifying such abuses. Without effective central government, many more abuses would be visited on the American people either by neglect or by other sources of concentrated power.

American progressives consider it necessary to avoid both the leftist extreme of state domination and the neo-rightist extreme of market domination, recognizing that the absence of government would abandon the fate of 270 million Americans to the interests of a handful of unaccountable giant multinational enterprises. Unlike libertarians and the Republican right, who argue that the state should shrink to its nineteenth-century proportions or even wither away, and unlike those who endow the state with a mystical general will that supersedes the diverse interests in society, progressives believe that government is an institution through which human needs can be satisfied and conflicts reconciled that could not be satisfied or reconciled by the unaided efforts of individuals, associations, local authorities, or market processes.

Politics within the framework of government is the art of managing differences in interests and values peacefully and non-coercively. Precisely because it is a human institution, government is vulnerable to imperfections and abuses; for that reason, its powers must be carefully circumscribed.

Thus, a democratic state (1) *exercises limited powers* constrained by law and an independent judiciary in order to protect the liberties of its citizens and to ensure the continuity of democratic institutions. Important spheres of life, notably religion, publishing, family relationships, recreation and entertainment, and organizational activities, should flourish independently of the state. The presumption should be that government does not abridge personal autonomy except for a compelling public interest, such as preventing child abuse or curbing racial, gender, or ethnic discrimination. (2) *Government* serves as an instrument available to society for the protection of life, property, security, and common values from external threats and internal abuses, and for providing useful services that, in the judgment of its elected officials, cannot be supplied on acceptable terms through market processes. (3) *Economic activity* is reserved to private enterprise, regulated primarily by market processes complemented by government action to compensate for market failures. (4) *Voluntary associations* based on religious, ethnic, neighborhood, occupational, or other ties are encouraged by government to provide for the mutual recreational, cultural, spiritual, charitable, protective, or political interests of their members, independently of government and of profit-seeking market processes. Autonomous citizen associations and activist government complement one another in maintaining vigorous democratic societies.[19] (5) Citizenship entails the acceptance by individuals, associations, and businesses of *responsibilities* to state and society, parallel to the rights with which all persons are endowed.

These are the five essential planks of the progressive platform and worldview.

I respect the Republican right for their effective strategy in gaining control of the agenda of American public life. Though their tactics have frequently been inept, mean-spirited, and self-defeating, exposing them to charges of callousness and extremism, their strategy of minimizing the role of government has been consistent and unrelenting.[20] My concern is that the structural changes and the policies they promote will create moral and political havoc in our nation unless they are curbed and reversed. Progressives of the moderate left and Democrats need both a convincing set of principles and a feasible strategy for reversing this threat. The purpose of this book is to supply them.

Civil Society and Globalization

Disenchantment with government during the final quarter of the twentieth century has produced two intellectual currents: it has led many to embrace competitive market processes, others to explore the viability of voluntary and cooperative associations. The latter are often referred to as components of civil society that serve as intermediaries between individuals and the state.[21] Each has spawned its armies of enthusiasts: partisans of civil society on the moderate left, of market capitalism on the right. Some argue that they should coexist in a productive, non-governmental division of labor; that is, tasks inappropriate for profit-seeking firms should be taken up by voluntary associations as government shrinks to its essentials—defense, police, and law enforcement.

My working premise is that many tasks that are essential to the maintenance and development of dynamic, complex, and just societies cannot be adequately performed in socially responsible ways either by private for-profit enterprises or by voluntary associations. They require the resources of government and the powers, including often the coercive powers, of the state restrained, however, by public accountability and by law.

My further premise is that coping with the needs of complex societies requires the activation of all its capacities for collective action: for-profit businesses, voluntary associations, and government. I reject the perverse zero-sum notion that these potential sources of collective energy must be inherently in conflict over turf. It is far more likely that in democratic systems such as the United States, they will work out complementary patterns of action in the form of network relationships, so that society may enjoy the fruits of their respective comparative advantages.[22]

This is the perspective that animates this volume. The emphasis is on government not because I regard for-profit enterprises or voluntary associations as undesirable or unimportant but because the systematic bashing that has been visited on government during the past two decades must be rectified, so that the American nation will not be deprived of the essential services that only activist government can provide.

The image of government propounded by the Republican right is that of an external, coercive imposition on society and markets that is prone to great mischief and even oppression and must consequently be rigorously restrained. Progressives hold a contrary vision. They view democratic government as an extension of American society, the most inclusive and comprehensive association that constitutes the American nation. There is no sharp dividing line between the U.S. government and the people. This government "of the people" expresses society's capacities to achieve common purposes that could not be accomplished by individuals or small groups. Whether it be flood control or national defense, Social Security or gun control, environmental protection or public education, the impulses normally originate in society and are converted by political struggle to the policies and programs of government. Should they fail to survive that struggle, they are modified or eliminated. When an established program loses public support, as in the cases of prohibition in the 1930s and welfare in the 1990s, it is amended, cut back, or terminated.

This radical divergence in their images of government is at the core of the contemporary conflict between rightists and progressives. As I share the progressives' faith in democratic government, this book is devoted to expounding that theme and demonstrating its relevance to the needs of American society on the brink of the third millenium.

Some readers may inquire at this point whether the current globalization of financial, production, and trading activities and of information has reduced government everywhere to virtual irrelevance. Would efforts to restore public confidence in the federal government and to recover its efficacy be doomed for that reason to futility? Are governments, including the government of the United States becoming, as we hear from enthusiasts for globalization, increasingly unnecesssary and irrelevant?

It is certainly true that, as a result of technological developments in communications systems and in transportation and the free-trade policies pursued since World War II by the United States and some of its allies, investment decisions, movements of capital, and production and distribution of many types of goods and services have become globalized. Such decisions are controlled by a small number of very large transnational firms and financial institutions whose primary concern is their own profitability, security, and market share. As communities and even governments compete for their favor in order to realize employment and tax benefits, these firms increasingly escape accountability to and regulation by any public authority. Since there seems little likelihood that one or more suprastate authorities will emerge with power to enact and enforce rules to govern the behavior of transnational firms, they are effectively accountable neither to national nor global public authority but only to the rules of competitive markets. Does globalization, therefore, herald an era of economic medievalism in which a handful of corporate barons, accountable only to themselves, write their own rules and operate in their own interest across territorial borders?

While this extreme version of globalization may be a caricature, it nevertheless reflects a reality to which governments must adapt. They must reconcile the need to provide a favorable climate for investment and operation with the need to protect demanding publics from some of the excesses and abuses—of labor standards, employment security, environmental hazards, consumer safety—to which some transnational enterprises are prone. Governments must continue to provide for national defense, enforce laws that protect life and property (including those of the transnationals), construct and maintain the physical infrastructure (including those that facilitate the operations of transnationals), and educate their youth (including those who staff the transnationals), maintain an environment of economic stability, and arrange for the decent and dignified care of those who are unable or no longer able to function as productive citizens.

To perform these essential functions, public revenues will continue to be required from individuals and businesses, including the transnationals. Thus, economic globalization will coexist uneasily with activist government. Citizens will continue to look to their government for services and protection that the transnationals do not provide and that individuals cannot manage for themselves, including help for disturbances in urbanized, mass societies undergoing rapid and often upsetting changes in economic and family structures and job opportunities. Neither in the United States nor in other democratic countries will the public accept the radical shrinking and disabling of government, the institution on which they have learned to rely for the satisfaction of some of their basic needs.

Bear in mind that markets, contrary to a rightist article of faith, are not natural phenomena. They are enabled and maintained by intricate legal arrangements and government policies that set and enforce rules for their operations. Where rulers, under public pressure, believe that unfettered globalization impairs vital interests of their constituents, they will move to constrain market operations within their borders, just as rightists in the United States propose to limit and criminalize pornography on the global Internet. In defiance of pressure from the United States, Japan and China persist with mercantilist economic policies. There are no guarantees that the European Union and Russia will accept unconstrained globalization if they believe their collective interests or those of significant constituencies, such as European farmers, are negatively affected. The refusal of the U.S. House of Representatives in the fall of 1997 to grant the president "fast track" authority to negotiate free trade agreements reflected the mobilization of widespread sentiment that unlimited and unreciprocated free trade inflicts unacceptable damage on important American publics. Although global markets are driven in part by technological developments, they are enabled and sustained only by conducive government policies. Small economies may have few alternatives but to accommodate to global markets, but large and rich economies such as the United States enjoy greater latitude. Their first duty remains the promotion and defense of the interests of their citizens, not of transnational corporations, and when these are believed to contradict the tenets of globalized markets, it is the latter that must yield.

There is little likelihood that governments, notably the government of the United States, will wither away under the impact of economic globalization. Globalization is a reality to which governments must respond and adapt but not yield. In many respects, globalization necessitates vigorous government both to complement the transnationals (to perform activities that are not profitable or that reflect societal values that cannot be accommodated by the profit motive); and to provide an essential source of countervailing power (to protect society from practices that may be profitable but that violate individual or community rights, values, or interests).[23]

CHAPTER TWO

Interests, Ideology, and Culture

Conservatives disagree on many issues, but the coalition unites them behind the goal of less government.

—Leslie Wayne, *New York Times*, July 8, 1997

The story of the conservative ascendency during the final quarter of the twentieth century—of which the anti-government theme is the central component—has been thoroughly recounted and documented and need not be revisited here.[1] Right-wing obsessions with "big government" as a liberal conspiracy are illustrated by the pundit George Will's revelation that the Clinton-Gore concerns with global warming and affirmative action are motivated by their desire to "extend government's reach deeper into Americans' lives."[2]

In addition to committed leadership and effective organization, a political movement as successful as the conservative ascendency depends on two factors: favorable circumstances (good timing) and loss of confidence among supporters of the status quo. The anti-government crusaders have been blessed on both counts.

Favorable Circumstances

The tragedy of the Vietnam War during the endless decade from the mid-1960s to the mid-1970s was the formative experience of the post–World War II generation. Among that cohort of educated American youth, which had previously supported active government in the spirit of John F. Kennedy as the instrument of racial justice, social progress, and the New Frontier, the federal government was transformed into a monster, waging brutal and meaningless, high-technology but incompetent warfare against a pathetic Third World people, while lying shamelessly to the American public and scheming to cover it up, as revealed in the *Pentagon Papers*.[3] Their growing cynicism was confirmed by President Nixon's lies and deceptions during the Watergate fiasco, demonstrating that at the highest levels, the federal government harbored a nest of unscrupulous conspirators constituting a threat to the constitutional order and the liberties of the American people. Vietnam and Watergate detached a generation of educated American youth from the liberal camp, conditioned them to cynical alienation from government, and prepared many for eventual acceptance of the anti-government, "conservative" creed.

The gains achieved by black Americans during this same period were perceived by large segments of the white working class, North as well as South, as a gratuitous, government-sponsored threat to their jobs, their neighborhoods, and the safety of their families. The civil rights movement and the federal legislation of the Johnson era, especially that pertaining to affirmative action, seemed calculated to advance the interests of blacks at the expense of patriotic white working men and their families who, faithful to America's individualist creed, had earned their positions, their status, and their property by virtue of hard work, without special help from government or the patronage of upper-class liberals. This sense of betrayal by the Democratic Party alienated large blocs of working-class Americans, who were among the staunchest supporters of the New Deal–Democratic coalition, from the forces that supported activist government.

The final blow that shattered the liberal coalition was the oil shock that triggered the recession of the mid- and late 1970s and the stagflation that bedeviled the Carter presidency. As real incomes declined with stagnant wages and double-digit inflation, as the federal government seemed unable to cope with this national "malaise," middle-class voters began to rebel against what they perceived to be unreasonably high taxes. Much of this revenue, they believed, was dissipated by incompetent and corrupt politicians on "welfare" to undeserving parasites who preferred to subsist on government handouts rather than work. "Tax-and-spend" liberals were wasting the people's hard-earned money on hare-brained schemes that did nothing for working Americans. These frustrations offered tempting targets to the well-financed apostles of minimal government and lower taxes and provided the Republican right with their most reliable campaign theme—lower taxes—for the next two decades.

The 1960s revolution in sexual behavior frightened and deeply offended large numbers of religiously oriented persons who believed that traditional Christian morality was the key to righteous individual living and the moral bedrock of genuine Americanism. Toleration of abortion, homosexuality, and explicit sex in the popular media, the judicial outlawing of prayer in public schools, draft dodging and the trashing of patriotism, and the promotion of racial equality were attributed to liberalism, the Democratic Party, and the federal government. Increasingly mobilized for political action by a new breed of televangelist preachers, they joined the ranks of the anti-government crusade, even though they were prepared to call on government, preferably state governments, to enforce their moral code.

The phenomenon of the "Reagan Democrats," who participated in Reagan's 1980 landslide victory, consisted of these disaffected elements: young people hoping for a fresh and more confident approach to the problems of government, working people rebelling against government-sponsored affirmative action combined with apparent government neglect of their concerns, middle-class voters demanding tax relief, and evangelical Christians protesting the collapse of traditional morality. Republicans maintained much of this support at the presidential level until 1992, when many of the same groups of voters defected to Clinton and Perot, enabling Clinton to prevail in a three-candidate race. By 1994 many were incensed by the image of sleaze among Democratic officeholders, including Clinton, and by his failure to deliver on his 1992 promises of tax relief, welfare reform, and health insurance. This resulted in the landslide that awarded Republicans control of Congress for the first time in forty years. Because Democrats, whose party was associated with active government, could not be trusted to keep their promises or even behave honestly in office, the Republican pledge of less and smaller government might be the answer.

Thus, the political recovery of the Republican right was abetted by favorable circumstances.

Loss of Confidence among Liberals

Events beyond their control shook liberals' confidence in their familiar prescriptions. To begin with, many were disillusioned with government as a consequence of Vietnam and Watergate and lost interest in public affairs. Moreover, their old, reliable prescriptions seemed no longer relevant. In the heyday of Keynesian economics, a ready solvent for economic recession was compensatory fiscal stimulus administered by expanding government expenditures. By the late 1970s, this became impossible. Inflation accompanying recession (stagflation) confounded this economic wisdom; clearly, fiscal stimulus was inappropriate medicine for an economy suffering from double-digit inflation. And when in 1981 a majority of the Democratic-controlled House of Representatives supported Reagan's massive tax cuts, which benefited primarily wealthy individuals and corporations, it became evident that the party of active government had run out of ideas, had lost confidence in its approaches to government, and in the party's ability to respond to the concerns of voters.

This was further demonstrated by the failure of Democrats and their intellectual supporters on the democratic left to address such problems as the declining supply of decent affordable housing for low-income working families; readjustment assistance for workers, their families, and their communities displaced by the transfer of jobs to low-wage sites overseas; the plight of the 40 million Americans subsisting in poverty and of the 40 million working Americans without health insurance; the redistribution of income in favor of the wealthy; the continuing stagnation and degeneration of the inner cities, even in times of relative prosperity; the massive fiscal and trade deficits that appeared to be entirely out of control; and fear that Japan had displaced the United States as the world's economic pacesetter. The intellectual hegemony of economic laissez-faire and minimal government in the mid-1990s was so complete that except for threats to the entitlements of large, middle-class constituencies (Medicare, Social Security), Democrats did not conceive, let alone propose federal initiatives that might alleviate such serious social and economic abuses, even when they controlled the Executive Branch. So eager were some of the "New Democrats" to pledge their allegience to the new orthodoxy that spokespeople for the Clinton White House dutifully pronounced their aversion to direct federal regulation and their commitment to "market methods," meaning, in the case of environmental goals, the trading of pollution credits.

Adding to the disarray of New Democrats has been the fragmentation of their supporters into single-issue constituencies, many of which are based on lifestyle rather than economic issues. These constituencies include the feminist bloc concerned with gender equality and abortion rights; the homosexual rights movement; the environmentalist and resource conservationist movements; racial and ethnic minorities, principally African Americans and Hispanics; and organized labor. Although all favor active government on behalf of their special causes, they have not combined into a winning coalition, nor do they invest in the Democratic Party as their political vehicle. And they omit many of the blue-collar and salaried working people that had been the core of the Roosevelt–Truman–Kennedy coalitions. President Clinton's success in 1992 required him to energize these diverse constituencies, while appealing successfully to middle-class voters on economic issues ("it's the economy, stupid!"). Clinton, however, has not attempted to offer a coherent rationale for active government. His inability or unwillingness to do so opened space for the Republicans in 1994 to win a massive victory with the most anti-government platform since the 1920s and to maintain control of Congress in 1996, despite Clinton's re-election.

Resources

The success of the anti-government forces has been achieved not only by favorable circumstances and the collapse of confidence among progressives but also by a set of resources that survived the mid-century era of active government and were available for exploitation and cultivation by the militant entrepreneurs of the Republican right. These resources can be summarized as interests, ideology, and culture.

Interests

The first of these resources are powerful interests, of which the most prominent and influential are corporate management and the wealthy owners of corporate assets. Though this core of American capitalism is highly diverse, with many specialized and often conflicting concerns, they have three common goals that unite them and bind them firmly to the minimal government camp. Thus, even when individual industries, such as mining, timber, cattle, and banking demand and struggle to preserve special government protection or subsidies, their hearts and their pocketbooks maintain their attachment to the principle of minimal government. Corporate management and their financial principals want (1) lower taxes on the incomes of businesses and wealthy individuals; (2) less government regulation of the environment, labor relations and labor standards, employment practices, consumer product safety, occupational health and safety, financial institutions, and securities markets; and (3) reduced government protection of labor unions.

Corporate ownership and management is firmly aligned with the Republican Party. In addition to impressive lobbying power, they contribute abundantly to Republican political campaigns in sums that enable the party and their candidates to dwarf their rivals. The more zealous among them sponsor and finance an impressive network of right-wing think tanks, foundations, and journals. The most prominent of the think tanks are the American Enterprise Institute; the Heritage, Bradley, and John M. Olin Foundations; the Cato and the Hoover Institutes; the Center for International and Strategic Studies; and the Federalist Society. Among the more influential journals are *National Review, American Spectator, Commentary,* and *Policy Review,* as well as the influential daily *Wall Street Journal.* These enable their sponsors and patrons to foster and sustain the community of sympathetic thinkers and writers who provide the intellectual firepower for the anti-government movement and campaigns. They also fund the political action cadres who produce press releases, place articles in friendly journals and mass media, and operate direct mailing services in close support of right-wing candidates and causes.

Right-wing foundations outspend their "liberal" rivals by an estimated margin of 4:1.[4] Even more important than the volume of funds, the major rightist foundations coordinate their efforts by focusing strategically on specific themes, issues, and targets as determined by their planning and coordinating agency, the Council on National Policy. By contrast, the progressively oriented foundations fragment their efforts over a wide range of causes with no common strategic focus. Their much sparser resources are diffused over many themes (feminism, environmentalism, labor, civil rights, gun control) with little awareness of the need to regard their activities as part of a common effort.

Thus, corporate management and their allies have enabled both the political activities and the intellectual offensive that account for the conservative ascendency of the past quarter century. In turn, Republican officeholders, in the judicial as well as the executive and legislative branches of the state and federal governments have been consistently responsive to the concerns of corporate management in the key areas of taxation, regulation, and labor relations. They have doggedly supported reductions in the capital gains and inheritance taxes, seriously proposed that self-regulation by industry better serves the public interest than government regulation of product safety, environmental abuses, and securities fraud, maintained a hostile attitude toward labor unions, and demonized "labor bosses."

Other interests are aligned with the anti-government movement. Among them are small businesses, strategically located on the main streets of every American community. They echo the grievances of corporate management against what they consider excessive taxation, burdensome, intrusive regulations, and aggressive labor unions. Prominent among these interests and among financial contributors to anti-government causes are the resource industries—timber, mining, oil, and cattle grazing—which fight to retain federal subsidies while seeking to roll back environmental and resource management regulations.

They are joined by the formidable gun lobby, which crusades against government regulation of ownership or sale of firearms as direct threats to their constitutionally guaranteed Second Amendment rights. The majority of Republicans in Congress have been united in their resistance to any and all measures that are found distasteful to the National Rifle Association. At the extreme of this large and well-organized anti-government coalition are the well-armed militia movements, which regard the federal government as part of a vast international conspiracy to subvert the liberties of American, white, Christian males and are prepared to resort to violent tactics, such as the Oklahoma City bombing, in defense of these liberties.

Christian evangelicals, mobilized for political action by a network of televangelist preachers, provide the Republican right with a large, active, and committed grassroots constituency. Unlike the business interests, their commitment to the anti-government cause is motivated less by economic concerns than by their conviction that the federal government, including the federal courts, (1) sponsors and protects immoral, anti-Christian behavior and practices such as abortion, pornography and homosexuality; (2) encroaches on their religious freedom by disallowing prayer in public schools and religious emblems in public buildings; (3) undermines family life by promoting gender equality and sexual promiscuity; and (4) "having let the Negroes into our schools and kept God out" penalizes Christian education by threatening to levy federal taxes on these institutions on the ground that their admissions practices discriminate against African-American children.

The Christian coalition has gained sufficient influence in Republican circles that it now controls the party machinery in a third of the states, has elected large numbers of local officials and school board members, and played a decisive role in drafting the party platform at the 1996 national Republican convention. Its activists lobby tirelessly at federal, state, and local levels for government vouchers that would channel public funds to private, including religious, schools. They associate active government with a godless and anti-Christian "secular humanism" that threatens their way of life. The Christian coalition frightens many moderate Republican and independent voters, but it provides the Republican right with its most active and devoted mass constituency.

On some of the causes for which the evangelists fight, such as government funds for private schools and the criminalization of abortion, they are joined by the Roman Catholic clergy. Unlike the Christian coalition, however, the Catholic clergy have not become an adjunct of the Republican Party; they favor government intervention on a number of issues that they associate with social and economic justice. Evangelicals complain that their contributions to the Republican cause are not matched by practical (as opposed to rhetorical) support by the Republican political leadership for measures that are dear to them, such as school prayer and criminalization of abortion, subordinating their concerns to those of the corporate elites. Yet, when their congressional leadership allowed themselves to be guided by the religious right, as in the impeachment of President Clinton (November 1998–February 1999), they suffered a humiliating defeat and a precipitous decline in public esteem.

Ideology

Ideology is the resource that rationalizes and justifies the specific programs and policies sponsored by the anti-government forces. The Republican right has embraced the principle that political behavior is determined not only by interests but also decisively by ideas. They believe that ideas matter and matter greatly, rejecting the comfortable liberal view that post–World War II prosperity had produced in the West the "end of ideology."[5] Motivated by this conviction, their core contributors have committed substantial funds to the elaborate infrastructure of think tanks, foundations, journals, and propaganda apparatus outlined earlier in this chapter, which maintains a large contingent of right-wing intellectuals, operates in close support of right-wing causes, and provides a *nomenclatura* of committed right wingers available for appointment to government positions. (Progressives have nothing to match it.) The components of this ideology have been in no sense original or creative. Instead, its proponents have exhumed and attempted to rehabilitate such late eighteenth- and nineteenth-century ideas as laissez-faire economics, social Darwinian morality, and states' rights politics and apply them to contemporary issues.

Competitive market economics is the centerpiece of the anti-government belief system. Central to that world view is the conviction that private enterprise, disciplined by competitive markets, is the engine that generates economic efficiency, consumer satisfaction and freedom of choice, social justice, and continuously expanding prosperity. It is ideally suited to the current era of globalized capitalism. Responding to the egoistic and materialistic nature of economic man, the pursuit of economic self-interest, driven by the profit motive, maximizes social welfare by virtue of the operation of the hidden hand, the legendary "magic of the market." Government interference, however well intentioned, distorts market outcomes by creating "rents" or unearned benefits through protection or subsidies that stifle entrepreneurial initiative, divert energies from creating wealth to political manipulation, and reward special interests at the expense of the rest of society. Competitive markets have the great virtue of correcting their own shortcomings and abuses, such as high prices or shoddy products, as more efficient competitors force enterprises to correct these abuses or drive them out of business.

The Republican right has embraced economic laissez-faire and free market fundamentalism, rejecting decades of experience and scholarship regarding the limitations of this model, which two generations ago appeared to be seriously flawed by the Great Depression of the 1930s.[6] Government regulation, promotion, and participation are to be eschewed as pernicious interference. Not only are governments likely to be incompetent and to serve as tools of special interests, but they are vulnerable to political corruption, plundering the enterprises that create the wealth of nations. Government activity should therefore be minimized. Government functions should, where possible, be privatized, divested to private interests or contracted for operation by private firms. Government programs that cannot be privatized should be compelled, where possible, to submit to economic competition by the introduction of "market surrogates" so that government will function as much as possible like private business. Government activity is condemned by the dread term, "socialism," even though Democrats have always been committed to free enterprise and the United States government, even at the height of the active government era in the 1960s, had a much smaller sector of its economy in government hands than any major industrial country.

Though the Republican right continue to identify themselves as "conservatives," their passionate embrace of free market fundamentalism has the unintended effect of transforming them into political and social radicals. In their present incarnation, nothing, certainly not government, must stand in the way of changes induced by the miracle of the market because, they believe, the long-run consequences will benefit all.[7] If market forces must disrupt families, devastate communities, foster monopoly, commercialize and coursen such human endeavors as education, sports, the fine arts, the national parks, and even religion, while promoting pornography and unrestrained violence in mass entertainment, all is well, all must be well because these consequences flow from the rational and inexorable logic of market processes. Democrats, strangely, have been cast in the role of conservatives, attempting to protect Social Security, Medicare, environmental protection, consumer safety regulations, and similar social controls from the the radical, Republican-inspired onslaughts of unregulated commercialism.[8]

Closely associated with laissez-faire ideology is the moral doctrine of social Darwinism. While Charles Darwin's thesis about the origin of species and the survival of the fittest pertain to the natural world, later thinkers, notably Herbert Spencer, extended its logic to apply to the human species, including competition among nations and races.[9] The competitive struggle for survival is part of a natural process that ensures the continuous health, adaptability, and renewal of the human species. Any interference by government in this natural process will have the perverse if unintended effect of thwarting these necessary processes of social adaptation and renewal, weakening the nation and the race.

From this struggle for existence, people tend to receive what they deserve. Those who thrive and prosper do so because of superior physical or intellectual endowments or their willingness to work hard and persevere; those who fail, the poor and the weaklings, the losers of this world, falter because of inferior genetic equipment, moral delinquency (drugs, alcohol, etc.), or sheer sloth. The need to struggle for livelihoods and for survival provides the necessary incentives for performance. If government intervenes, by welfare or other palliatives, it undermines these incentives and contributes to the degeneration of individual nations and eventually the human species. Any sentiments of compassion for the suffering or plight of the weak and fallen, however commendable on moral grounds, should be expressed through religious institutions and private charity (President Bush's "thousand points of light").

Through the course of American history, those who have opposed social change or effective government action on any subject from slavery to child labor, environmental protection, or gun control have resorted to the doctrine of states' rights. Thus, it is not surprising that the current generation of skeptics has followed suit: any activity that must be performed by government should be the responsibility, where possible, of the several states. Activities "usurped" by the federal government during the era of active government should be privatized or devolved to the states.

The anti-government forces of the late twentieth century have exhumed the anti-federalist tirades of the late 1780s, which condemned the proposed Constitution as replacing the British monarchy with a centralized republican tyranny.[10] In that same spirit, the present generation of states' righters argue that the fifty states are the natural tribunes of their residents, close to their distinctive needs and preferences, sensitive to and responsive to their demands, unlike the remote, impersonal, and unaccountable Washington bureaucrats. Individual citizens are said to identify with and owe primary allegiance to their respective state governments. Representatives of the Republican right, including a majority of the Supreme Court appointed by Presidents Reagan and Bush, have rediscovered the Tenth Amendment to the Constitution, which reserves unenumerated powers to the states and the people, conveniently ignoring two centuries of constitutional interpretation by the courts beginning with the redoubtable, arch-conservative Chief Justice John Marshall.[11] States' rights once again are being deployed as an ideological weapon to discredit and disable the federal government.

A final component of the rightist ideological repertoire combines, not always comfortably, the themes of radical individualism and traditional morality. Every person must make his or her way in the world; those who succeed have a moral right to retain and enjoy the fruits of their success; those who fail have no reasonable expectation of outside help except through private charity; government has no right or obligation to intervene. Traditional morality enjoins the individual to adhere to the Ten Commandments, with special emphasis on sexual abstinence outside marriage and the expectation that delinquent behavior, including homosexuality and abortion (murder of the innocent unborn fetus), should be proscribed, criminalized, and punished by government. Tensions arise between the self-absorbed individualism and hedonism implied in the first of these themes and the moral restraints on individual behavior that follow from the second. The reconciliation of these two themes, each of which commands an important constituency in the anti-government coalition, remains an unresolved challenge for rightist political managers. What binds them into an effective political force is their common hostility to the role of government in economic affairs.[12]

What I have outlined above is the worldview, the vision of the America that the current generation of rightist thinkers aspires to create. A progressive worldview, by contrast, would agree that profit-seeking free enterprise in competitive markets, supported by a governmental network of laws, policies, and services, yields unparalleled levels of productivity and economic efficiency. The distribution of the resulting economic abundance, however, is the problem they address, as unregulated market processes yield not only expanding inequality but also often harsh injustice, insecurity, and needless human suffering. Although economic associations such as labor unions and cooperatives wielding countervailing power can mitigate some of these excesses, the main instrument available to society for realizing greater social justice and more genuine equality of opportunity is democratic government. Thus, the framers of the Constitution created a government to "establish justice" and "promote the general welfare."

The responsibility of such a government is to ensure patterns of distribution that maintain incentives to economic efficiency (thus substantial inequality of wealth and incomes), while providing to all citizens who are willing and able to work the minimum needed for secure, decent family livelihoods and dignified old age. In addition, government regulation must curb monopoly and the abuses of unregulated profit seeking by protecting the natural environment, the safety of consumer products, decent and safe working conditions, the integrity of financial institutions, and non-discriminatory employment, housing, and educational practices. It should ensure the availability of high-quality, free public education and access to health services for all members of society. Even though personal morality, including sexual behavior, are private matters beyond the legitimate reach of government, self-regarding individualism must be tempered by the realization that the security and well-being of each depend on fairness to all and on a public interest that transcends the claims of individuals. This, in brief, is the contrasting progressive vision for America's future, an alternative ideology. Its realization requires energetic action by the federal government, supplementing similar initiatives by voluntary citizens' associations and by state and local governments.[13]

An important current in the Western philosophical tradition is the notion of "higher law," a set of principles originating either in divine sanction (the law of God) or in nature (natural law) with which the enactments of governments must comply if they are to retain their legitimacy. When the behavior of governments flouts higher law (as did the actions of the British Parliament, according to the Declaration of Independence), individuals are no longer morally bound to obey them and may be entitled to resist, by violent means if necessary. Both rightists and progressives appeal to higher law regarding values that are important to them: rightists to protect traditional morality and free enterprise, progressives to protect First Amendment rights and individual privacy.

On the fringes of both camps, some are prepared to resort to disobedience and even violence. This included, among leftists, antiwar protesters during the Vietnam War. Among rightists are antigovernment fanatics, including members of the militia movements, who preach and sometimes practice disobedience (e.g., refusing to pay federal taxes) and violence (such as the Oklahoma City bombing). Certain cultish movements circulate rumors of conspiracies fomented by the federal government in league with powerful, secretive, exotic and satanic elements to impose foreign rule on the American people and deprive them of their liberties. These fantasies are abetted in academic circles by devotees of the postmodernist cult that rejects the need for empirical validation of ideas and regards all claims to truth, especially from non-establishment sources, as plausible.[14]

In this book I have avoided the term "liberal" to identify contemporary partisans of activist government because "liberal" has become identified with multiple and contradictory meanings. Originally, in the tradition of John Locke and John Stuart Mill, liberalism connoted the protection of individual freedom (inalienable rights) from the intrusion of government, especially in matters of belief, expression, and economic activities. Beginning in the early years of the twentieth century, with the American progressives and the British Liberals under Lloyd-George, its meaning was modified to encompass the extension of individual liberty and security by the positive intervention of government. Wilson's New Freedom and FDR's New Deal, with their activist mission for government, transformed the popular understanding of "liberal."

Twentieth-century liberalism shared with the older tradition its suspicion of government interference in matters of belief, expression, and other First Amendment rights, while it deviated from that tradition by advocating a positive role for government in social and economic affairs. To illustrate the confused meaning of the term "liberal," the current set of economic policies intended to minimize the role of government in economic management—privatization, deregulation, marketization—is referred to as neo-liberalism. To avoid this semantic confusion, I employ the term "progressive" to designate a set of values, an approach to public affairs, and guidelines for socioeconomic policies that favor activist government. This is faithful to the progressive tradition in American political experience.

Culture

The third resource available to the Republican right is a deep strain of popular culture that is suspicious, cynical, and fearful of public authority, especially of government that is not immediately accountable to local communities. The lessons of "eternal vigilance" as the price of liberty; of life, liberty, and the pursuit of happiness without interference by public authority as the inalienable birthright of every American; of "government is best that governs least" have been drilled into American schoolchildren since the founding of the Republic. Individual liberty is the leitmotiv of the American sense of self. The principal threat to that liberty, according to the nation's founding myth, today as under George III, is central government. Government is a necessary evil that must be endured, more a burden than a benefit, and its exactions, including taxation, must be kept to an irreducible minimum. Although particular government programs may be greatly appreciated (e.g., Social Security, interstate highways, disaster relief, national parks), they are regarded as exceptions to the general rule that government, chiefly the federal government, tends to impinge on the liberties of citizens and needs to be carefully circumscribed. As freedom is the possession of natural rights by individuals, it takes precedence over their responsibilities to society or even to fellow citizens. When individual rights clash with claims on behalf of society, the burden of proof is on the need for such claims (e.g., environmental protection, gun control, labor standards) that would limit the exercise of individual rights. This issue pertains especially to property rights.[15]

Whereas our neighbors to the north established their Confederation in 1867 to ensure "peace, order, and good government," ours has surrounded government with numerous checks and controls in order to glorify the individual and ensure his or her liberty against the inherent and inevitable abuses of central government. That every individual should be free to pursue happiness and must be master of his or her own fate—the key principles of the dominant Protestant tradition—were reenforced by the frontier experience. The rugged individualism of frontier life, where the individual pioneer conquered the wilderness without outside help, was early converted into a set of myths that circulated widely throughout the country and abroad, influencing the attitudes and expectations of multitudes, including many who never knew the frontier at first hand. Well into the twentieth century, after the United States had become an urbanized society, the dominant hero type in popular fiction and cinema was the lone individual (Gary Cooper, James Stewart, John Wayne) who stood up for liberty and justice against the unscrupulous machinations of greedy interests protected by corrupt governments and venal politicians. Politicians are the butt of popular humor—blunderers, time-servers, and, more than likely, crooks. "Bureaucrat" has become a term of opprobrium and derision, denoting faceless, unaccountable and mostly useless men and women who draw comfortable salaries but return little service to the hard-pressed taxpayer.

There is a powerful strain of populism in American political culture, glorifying the inherent wisdom and moral rectitude of ordinary people. Their sound judgment, based on living experience and common sense, is believed to be a more reliable guide to public policy than the bloodless calculations of experts insulated in their offices or laboratories or the outcomes of deliberative processes in the institutions of government, vulnerable as they are to the machinations of special interests and the manipulations of corrupt politicians. Though institutions are vulnerable to corruption, the people remain rock solid. "The people, yes!" [16]

The Progressives' campaign in the early years of the twentieth century for the initiative, referendum, and recall reflected this lack of confidence in elected politicians and the institutions of representative government. The current campaigns for term limitations and a balanced budget amendment to the Constitution, combined with limitations on congressional taxing power, demonstrate the persistence of this attitude. Distrust of and contempt for government is common fare within the commercial mass media; for example, see the television network features such as "The Fleecing of America," the popular radio programs of the commentators Rush Limbaugh and Howard Stern, the newspaper columns of the essayists George Will and William Safire, and the entertainment provided by such comedians as P. J. O'Rourke. [17]

In their campaign to demonize and discredit the federal government, the Republican right has been able to tap and exploit this prominent theme in American elite and popular culture. In an extreme form, this set of attitudes is manifested in the militia cult which, as previously observed, perceives the federal government as an imminent threat to American liberties. This doctrine has been especially attractive to many white males whose status in life has fallen short of their expectations and who are looking for scapegoats. They are attracted to organizations sponsored by white supremacists, neo-Nazis, and other anti-Semites. [18] Members of the public, already conditioned by the culture into which they have been socialized to suspect government and distrust politicians, are easy targets for the unremitting barrage of messages that expound these themes and for politicians who plead for electoral support along these same lines.

There is, however, a contrary strain of popular culture identified by the historian Daniel Boorstin as the "improving spirit" that can be traced back to the New England Puritans and that, like a dormant volcano, reemerges from time to time as a powerful influence on public policy.[19] Confidence that the world can be made better, that abuses can be corrected, that reality can be brought closer to aspirations and ideals by citizen initiative has been and remains a centerpiece of the progressive vision. The forebearers of this generation of progressives during such periods as the Progressive movement early in the twentieth century and during the Kennedy-Johnson years fought for and eventually achieved such reforms as the eight-hour day and the minimum wage, conservation of natural resources and environmental protection, women's rights and the civil rights laws, free trade unions, Social Security, and a merit-based civil service. All were launched as citizen movements and finally gained the endorsement and patronage of government, after long struggles and in the face of bitter opposition and sneering attacks on their proponents as "do gooders" and even subversives. The tradition of the improving spirit, that what is right and good can be made manifest in this world, of citizen-based social reform, has been eclipsed during the current conservative anti-government ascendency, but it continues to animate progressive thought and progressive political activity.

Disillusionment with active government, beginning with the Vietnam War and Watergate, the protracted, bitter controversy over affirmative action, and the economic malaise of the late 1970s stripped away support from the progressive approach to public affairs that favored active government, undermined the self-confidence and even the convictions of many erstwhile supporters, and opened political space for revitalized, militant apostles of minimal government. The Republican right nurtured, cultivated, and drew skillfully from the rich but dormant resources available to them—powerful and well-heeled *interests*, well-established sets of *ideas*, and deep-seated *cultural traditions*. From a historical perspective, this should come as no surprise, since the American experience has been characterized by alternating cycles of active government, followed by periods of reaction that cut back and sharply limit its scope.[20]

CHAPTER THREE

The American Experience
with Government

The tradition of affirmative government is quite as authentically
American, quite as deeply ingrained in our national history, quite as
strongly identified with our greatest statesmen, quite as expressive
of American ideas and character, as the competing tradition of self-
interest and scrambling private enterprise.
    —Arthur M. Schlesinger Jr., *The Cycles of American History*

What can be considered "normal" in American experience, an enduring theme of its basic culture as outlined in chapter 2, is suspicion of
public authority, especially of the federal government. This attitude is
reenforced by the devotion to liberty and the radical individualism that
are the bedrock themes of the American creed. Therefore, during good
times, when the economic indices are pointing upward, the normal
dominates the public agenda. Private enterprise is diffusing relative
well-being. There is no national crisis, nor are there widespread grievances that compel intervention by the federal government. Diffuse dis-
content is muted by prosperity, even though hard times may persist
for substantial groups, such as farmers during the 1920s or unskilled
and semi-skilled workers during the 1980s and 1990s. Taxes and regulations that once seemed necessary are perceived by dominant opinion makers as less and less tolerable. Services that once commanded
majority support are safely cut back or eliminated as needless drains
on the Treasury. Attention is focused on abuses perpetrated by politicians and bureaucrats identified with Washington, rather than on unmet needs or shortcomings of the capitalist establishment. With less
evident need for government, its role can be cut back and "normalcy"
restored.

With national crisis—war, the threat of war, or economic depression—or the accumulation of unattended needs and grievances, the
cycle is renewed. Only the federal government is equipped to cope

with such emergencies. At such times, it is pressed to activate hitherto dormant powers and claim required resources. In turn, the dominant mood of the public shifts, accepting as necessary an expanded role for government, eclipsing for the time being contrary voices warning of the dangers of big government to individual liberty. The momentum of activist government may then extend to a wide range of issues not previously addressed by federal authority.

Then, as the sense of crisis begins to dissipate, as grievances multiply against excesses or abuses of federal authority, opponents of federal power find fresh audiences, and the cycle is renewed. The antigovernment mood takes over, the role of the federal government is restrained, taxes are reduced, and the ideology of unconstrained market liberalism takes on new life. Each successive period of relatively activist or passive federal power creates the conditions that eventually supplant it. In the former case, controversies created by new federal programs or excesses and abuses of government powers discredit the notion of activist government. In the latter case, compelling public needs that have been denied or unaddressed generate irresistible demands for government initiatives.

Cycles, however, are not the whole story. After each successive episode of expansion, the federal government never contracts to its previous dimensions. There is always a residue of activities that become permanent federal programs because of a consensus that they are useful and needed or because of the pressure of supportive constituencies. Thus, there has been a secular growth in the range of federal functions — of services and regulations. This steady accretion of functions can be attributed less to the machinations of self-serving politicians and ambitious bureaucrats, or to the power of greedy "special interests" or to collusion among them, as to the exigencies of an increasingly complex, interdependent, urbanized society and economy compounded by America's ascendency to world power and, more recently, to superpower status. Although the percentage of GDP that is taken and allocated by the federal government never returns during each reversion to "normalcy" to the nadir of the previous cycle, the federal share of GDP at the end of the twentieth century, about 20 percent, remains substantially lower than that of any industrialized country, save Japan, and would be considerably lower still were it not for our defense commitments. After the Cold War, these exceed the combined defense expenditures of all our European allies plus Russia.[1]

Thus, the popularity of government and the functions it performs have risen and receded over the history of the Republic in a pattern described in further detail below. Like the ebb and flow of the tides on some shores, each rising tide leaves a deposit that becomes a permanent part of the shoreline, configuring it over time along new lines. The periodization is not rigid, because of the numerous interests that continue to exert their political and intellectual influence on government at the federal and state levels. Although this periodization denotes the dominant trend during each cycle, some of these influences may be contrary to the prevailing mood of their era.

Launching the Republic: The Federalist Years, 1787–1801

The Constitution of 1787–89 was a nationalizing document. Its first objective was to "form a more perfect union." The delegates to the Philadelphia convention were selected by the thirteen state legislatures which, in turn, were called upon to ratify the completed draft, but it was promulgated in the name of "we, the people of the United States," who distributed the powers of government among federal and state authorities. Because the Constitution was understood as a centralizing instrument, it drew the determined opposition of anti-federalists, whose hostility to activist government as expressed in numerous acerbic pamphlets and newspapers is replicated two centuries later in similar attacks on the federal government and its initiatives.[2] In deference to their concerns, the First Congress enacted and the states promptly ratified the Bill of Rights, the first ten amendments, of which the tenth reserves to the states and the people those powers not granted to the federal government.

During the critical first decade of the Republic, the government was in the hands of committed nationalists led by Secretary of the Treasury Alexander Hamilton. Hamilton promoted the principle of "energetic" government, including an activist foreign policy that would promote American security and commercial interests, by force if necessary, against all comers. As spokesman for the eastern banking, trading, and manufacturing interests, Hamilton contrived to ensure the new government's credit by assuming the debts of the thirteen states, providing for a strong and stable currency, and establishing the Bank of the United States. As a mercantilist and economic nationalist, he proposed in his celebrated *Report on Manufactures* (1791) to promote economic development by a protective tariff on manufactured products, and to facilitate internal trade by improving harbors and constructing canals and turnpikes. He led a military expedition against the "Whiskey Rebellion" in western Pennsylvania to suppress a local challenge to the federal taxing power. One of the lasting contributions of the founding generation of federalists was the appointment of the redoubtable John Marshall, whose thirty-five years as Chief Justice established a firm juridical basis for legitimizing the exercise of "implied powers" that expanded the scope of federal authority and activist government, while nullifying measures by state governments that encroached on federal powers.[3]

The Jeffersonian Era, 1801–1816

Jefferson's accession to the presidency was a decisive populist rejection of activist government which, he believed, operated on behalf of the economic elites. Jefferson believed that a wholesome republic must be based on self-reliant, property owning, white yeoman farmers free to manage their own affairs. In the tradition of John Locke and his eighteenth-century disciples, Jefferson's passionate commitment to individual liberty, especially in matters of religion, produced his opposition to government intervention in the lives of citizens. His suspicion of government intervention was further confirmed by Hamilton's patronage of the rich and the well born. While recognizing the necessity of manufacturing development, Jefferson distrusted bankers, financial manipulators, and commodity speculators as parasites who exploited the honest labors of productive workers. Aside from protecting the liberties of free citizens, government should govern as little as possible, he believed, and preferably at state and local levels, where it would be directly accountable to the people and reflect their needs and interests. At the ideological level, Jefferson and his followers emphasized states' rights over national powers and the interests of farmers, craftsmen, and debtors over those of capitalists and bankers.

Jefferson, however, was no extremist on these issues, since he visualized a spacious republic and unhesitatingly used federal powers to double the size of the new nation by negotiating the Louisiana Purchase, which he financed by expanding the federal debt. He also supported the proposals of his visionary treasury secretary, Albert Gallatin, for a comprehensive, federally financed network of roads and canals.[4] From the birth of the nation, the vast territories of the public domain beyond the boundaries of the original states were controlled and managed by the federal government. Even after new states had been admitted to the union, the federal government continued to own the public domain. "The Federal government, not the new western states or the operations of the market, fixed the terms on which settlers could acquire their lands."[5] The new landowners expected government to protect them from hostile foreigners and Indians and to help them increase the value of their land by providing transportation facilities and other improvements.

Like Jefferson, his friend and successor, James Madison, was a strict constructionist opposed to the expansion of federal activities. Yet circumstances, including interference with U.S. shipping and the forced impressing of U.S. sailors into the Royal Navy, compelled him to launch the costly and indecisive War of 1812 against Great Britain. Though New England federalists opposed the war as detrimental to their economic interests and even threatened at the 1814 Hartford Convention to secede from the union, the war had a nationalizing effect. Expenditures for waging the war imposed heavy burdens on the national credit that necessitated the chartering of the second Bank of the United States in 1816.

The American System, 1816–1829

The Jeffersonian mood was superseded by the more expansive demands of the "American system," a set of nationalist aspirations enunciated by the political titans of the era, Henry Clay and Daniel Webster. They represented a coalition that united the bankers and manufacturers of the East Coast with frontier developers, contractors, and land speculators who demanded federal help in suppressing and expelling the Indian tribes and in constructing canals and turnpikes that would facilitate the movement of goods and of settlers to the new lands beyond the Appalachians. Manufacturers secured tariffs (the "tariff of abominations") in 1828 to protect so-called infant industries from foreign imports. President John Quincy Adams argued forcefully for an activist federal government to promote economic development and the sciences, including the establishment of a national university. The mood of activist government dominated the several states as well, including the chartering of numerous banks and corporations and the awarding of monopoly privileges to build and operate transportation facilities. During this period, the state of New York built the Erie Canal, which transported thousands of settlers safely and cheaply to the Great Lakes and the upper Midwest. Pennsylvania responded with the Philadelphia-Pittsburgh turnpike and canal.

Minimal Federal Power and States' Rights, 1829–1861

During the three decades that preceded the Civil War, a new coalition emerged of slaveholders and backwoods farmers who were hostile both to federal power and the influence of the northeastern economic elites. The status of slavery dominated public policy. Slave interests suspected that the federal government would serve as the instrument of those who aimed to limit the spread to slavery and even to abolish it. In control of the southern and border states, of the Democratic Party, and of the U.S. Senate, they contrived to restrain the scope of federal activity and to argue passionately for states' rights. As producers and exporters of agricultural products and importers of manufactured goods, they opposed protective tariffs and succeeded in 1832 and 1833 in substantially reducing the tariff schedules.

In 1836, during the presidency of Andrew Jackson, the hero of the backwoods farmers, the charter of the Bank of the United States was allowed to expire, since it was charged with serving special interests at the expense of ordinary productive citizens. Government intervention, especially provisions that authorized corporations, was vulnerable to similar charges. These same special interests were blamed for the banking crisis and the depression of 1837. When the federal treasury enjoyed a surplus of revenues, President Jackson and Congress preferred to distribute it to the states rather than finance federal projects.[6] The northern and eastern industrial interests, now outvoted in Washington, shifted their focus to state government. It should be noted, however, that despite their commitment to states' rights, the plantation interests were prepared to call on federal powers to fight the Mexican War (and thus extend the domain of slavery) and to enforce the Fugitive Slave Law.

During the decade of the 1850s, Washington was paralyzed by its inability to resolve the conflicting pressures of slave interests and northern Free Soilers. With the future of the union at stake, the crisis came to a head with the election of Lincoln to the presidency in 1860.

Civil War and Reconstruction, 1861–1877

The election of Lincoln and the secession of the slave states in 1861 radically shifted the balance of power in Washington to the North and the East and from slaveholders and their allies to industrialists and land speculators who desired tariff protection and the aggressive development and settlement of the West. The Civil War required the conscription of manpower and the unprecedented mobilization of material resources that greatly expanded the scope and scale of federal activity.[7] As the war raged, Congress abandoned the gold standard, increased tariffs on manufactured goods, established a system of federally chartered national banks to facilitate the mobilization of capital and marketing of the national debt, provided for the distribution of federal lands in the West to homesteaders on generous terms, and made large land grants available to subsidize railway construction and to establish a college in each state to teach agricultural sciences and the mechanic arts.[8] After the fighting stopped in 1865, federal authority was extended to "reconstruct" the rebel states, to ensure that newly enacted laws to protect the civil rights and the voting privileges of emancipated negroes were enforced. Amendments were added to the federal Constitution that abolished slavery, extended federal and state citizenship to former slaves, required state governments to provide equal protection of the laws, and entrenched the voting rights of former slaves.

The Civil War and its aftermath expanded the federal role to new dimensions before the abuses, corruption, and high costs associated with Reconstruction combined with pressure from the New South created a reaction that terminated the military occupation of the former Confederate states, returning economic and political dominance to the next generation of the southern gentry. Finance capital, which had expanded and prospered during the war, lost confidence in the ability of the Treasury to manage the nation's finances and successfully campaigned for restoration of the gold standard.

The robber baron era witnessed the ascendency in American public life of two closely associated doctrines, economic laissez-faire and social Darwinism. Except for tariffs to protect the domestic market, manufacturers and their allies shifted directions, concluding that the need for active government on their behalf was less pressing than their interest in restraining government "interference" in their operations, such as regulating the terms and conditions of employment, monopolistic price setting, manipulation of securities, and other measures that might limit their freedom of entrepreneurial action and increase their tax obligations. This was the Gilded Age, during which many of America's great family fortunes were accumulated, often by predatory and monopolistic practices, and by resistance to the feeble efforts by the federal government (e.g., the Interstate Commerce Commission, formed in 1887, and the Sherman Anti-Trust Law, enacted in 1890) to restrain these practices. This era witnessed unprecedented concentrations of wealth and economic power, the growth of urban centers with large factories and mills manned by recent immigrants working long hours under harsh and often unsafe conditions for meager wages, and widespread distress among yeoman farmers, especially in the Midwest. The structural elements of large-scale industrialization and urbanization and the social conflicts they incubated began to confront the nation.

Bribing politicians and contributing large sums to candidates for public office to purchase their compliance or special favors were institutionalized as business practices during this period. These trends were abetted by the federal courts, which for three quarters of a century, beginning about 1870, enforced the sanctity of property rights and laissez-faire economics, and narrowly circumscribed the scope of federal and state regulation or service provision in social and economic affairs.[9]

As political spokesmen for the dominant industrial and financial circles of the Northeast and Midwest, Republicans reversed the position of their Federalist and Whig forebears and the founders of their party, who had favored activist government. Some Democrats, in turn, as spokesmen for rural debtors, unskilled workers, and recent immigrants, shifted from their previous aversion to federal intervention and began to espouse cautious measures of government-sponsored reform, such as the expansion of bank credit and the free coinage of silver, to ease the plight of farmers and other debtors, and the eight-hour day, to improve the lot of manufacturing and railroad workers and miners. Because Democrats were also the vehicle of the southern gentry, which continued to espouse states' rights, and of a gold-standard contingent based in the Northeast, they were ineffective in promoting any significant social or political reforms. Although socialist parties based on appeals to working-class solidarity and government ownership of the means of production emerged during this period as political forces throughout Europe, they never achieved more than marginal status in this country.

As the party that won the Civil War, Republicans were solicitous of an important mass constituency—the veterans of the Grand Army of the Republic and their widows and children. In violation of their social Darwinian ethos, they initiated a program of federal pensions for GAR veterans and family members. For half a century, these benefits served as the Republicans' principal pork barrel and the first large-scale welfare program in the American experience.[10]

The Progressive Era, 1900–1921

The accumulated neglect of the three post–Civil War decades and the numerous grievances that followed in their wake produced the inevitable reaction in public policy and a much more conducive intellectual and political climate for activist government. Muckraking journalists exposed the abuses of unregulated capitalism such as ruthless monopoly, exploited labor, unsafe food products, and threats to the public health, and the corrupt practices of urban machine politics. A new generation of upper-middle-class publicists and social reformers demanded federal action to redress these abuses and restore virtue to American public life—and, for the new nationalists among them, to guide America's ascendency to world-power status. The Progressive thinkers of that era were convinced that an active federal government was required to restore wholesome morality to a civilization that had been corrupted by the aggressive cupidity of the robber barons and the venality of their political allies.[11]

The Progressive movement was catalyzed politically by the powerful personality of an aristocrat turned maverick Republican, Theodore Roosevelt. As the dominant political force during the first decade of this century, he drove a reluctant Republican establishment to acquiesce in a number of measures that ran against their grain. He sponsored and dramatized highly publicized "trust busting" (enforcement of the hitherto moribund Sherman Anti-Trust Law), supported the creation of national parks and forests (conservation of natural resources), advocated professionalizing the Executive Branch by expanding the coverage of civil service laws, and in general, drew on federal power to counteract the abuses of concentrated economic power ("the malefactors of great wealth"). Above all, Roosevelt was an aggressive nationalist, a believer in America's "manifest destiny" as an imperial power.[12] He expanded the U.S. Navy to claim the status of a world power, seized the Panama Canal Zone and built the Panama Canal, and mediated the settlement of the Russo-Japanese war—all of which enhanced America's international status and the role of the federal government.

A brief reaction during the Taft administration was followed by the eight-year Democratic presidency of Woodrow Wilson, which renewed the momentum of the Progressive movement. Both Roosevelt and Wilson were committed to the principle and practice of presidential leadership and an activist federal government.[13] Whereas Roosevelt was an unabashed statist, an admirer and biographer of Alexander Hamilton, Wilson emphasized the use of federal power to protect individual rights. During his presidency, the Federal Trade Commission was established to protect consumers, a federal income tax was legitimated by a constitutional amendment, as was the direct election of U.S. senators, and the Federal Reserve Board was introduced to serve as an embryonic central bank. In 1917 Wilson led the country into the First World War, which expanded federal management of the economy to ensure the supply of munitions and war matériel. Conscription was introduced to mobilize the required manpower, and the railroads were taken over, for the duration, by the government. America's participation in the war ended with the Armistice in November 1918, followed by rapid demobilization and the dismantling of wartime controls. The Senate rejected U.S. membership in Wilson's League of Nations project, as the national mood quickly reverted to isolationism.

The Roaring Twenties

The Republicans swept back to power after the presidential and congressional elections of 1920, determined to revert to "normalcy," that is, to laissez-faire economic policy, social Darwinism, passive government, and isolationism. The first eight years were a period of unprecedented economic boom and high prestige for American capitalism. The federal government was in the hands of men committed to low taxes, minimal government, and the beneficent effects of self-regulating markets. Though agriculture was in a state of chronic depression, industry flourished behind high tariff walls, which Republican apologists managed to reconcile with their minimal government ideology. They also promoted and enforced national prohibition on the manufacture and sale of alcoholic beverages, in deference to the Protestant and rural constituencies that remained mainstays of Republican support.

During the final few years of this era, beginning with the stock market crash of October 1929, the country lapsed into the most severe economic depression in its history. Unemployment (25 percent of the labor force), bankruptcies, home and farm mortgage foreclosures, and bank failures reached all-time highs. Though public confidence in the capitalist economy collapsed in the face of widespread suffering and despair brought on by the depression, the Republican leadership clung to their conviction that the markets would eventually correct themselves, that government interference and efforts to stimulate economic activity and mitigate suffering would only make matters worse. President Hoover assured the American people that prosperity was "just around the corner" and that the American people would gain moral strength from overcoming the hardships of the depression experience.[14]

The New Deal and the Great Society, 1933–1969

The havoc and suffering wrought by the Great Depression shook American confidence in unregulated capitalism. The public, including many business leaders, turned to the federal government and demanded urgent action. Franklin D. Roosevelt's New Deal experimentation with government intervention to promote economic recovery, reduce unemployment, support farm prices, underwrite home and farm mortgages, protect investors and bank depositers, initiate welfare measures such as Social Security, finance huge public works such as the Tennessee Valley Authority and numerous labor-intensive local Works Progress Administration (WPA) improvements, support the rights of labor unions, and initiate crude attempts at macro-economic management transformed the nation's conception of the appropriate role of the federal government. The Republican Party survived Roosevelt's overwhelming reelection victory in 1936 as a small fragment in Congress. Shortly after that election, the Supreme Court, which had declared several New Deal initiatives unconstitutional, changed direction and accepted an expanded role for the federal government in economic and social affairs.

The New Deal, which established the federal government as the nation's paramount problem solver, was followed by preparation for and participation in World War II. During this national crisis, which lasted for five years, the nation's human and material resources were stretched and regimented by the federal government as never before, culminating in total victory in Europe and the Pacific. By bipartisan agreement, the traditional policy of isolationism was set aside in favor of vigorous world leadership and international cooperation.

Hardly had the public begun to relax and resume the accustomed peacetime rhythms than the Cold War ensued between the United States and the Soviet Union, the major victors in World War II. The Marshall Plan was implemented and NATO was launched to protect Western Europe from Soviet subversion and expansion. The Cold War endured for forty years, punctuated by vicious local wars in Korea and Vietnam, requiring the maintenance of a large national security establishment with associated defense contractors and scientific networks, all financed and directed from Washington. Many of the product innovations in American industry for the balance of the century could be traced to technological breakthroughs sponsored by the military establishment and the various space programs.

Except for a two-term interregnum under the Republican moderate and war hero Dwight Eisenhower, Democrats controlled the executive branch of the federal government during the third of a century from Roosevelt-Truman through Kennedy-Johnson. Congress was in their hands for thirty-two of these thirty-six years. During his eight years in office, Eisenhower, though uninterested in extending New Deal reforms, made few efforts to roll them back, while leaders of the dominant East Coast business establishment believed that big government and strong labor unions were the price they must pay for continued prosperity, social stability, and international leadership.

During Kennedy's brief presidency, his enthusiasm for public service, along with his sponsorship of the Peace Corps and VISTA (Volunteers in Service to America), set the optimistic tone for the New Frontier. During the latter years of the Kennedy-Johnson era, the federal government championed the civil rights movement, which attempted to vindicate the rights of America's racial minorities, supported the campaign for gender equality, and launched Johnson's ill-fated War on Poverty. While industry, agriculture, and finance prospered in private hands, there was hardly a dimension of American life that was unaffected by government services or regulation. State and local government expanded in tandem with the federal, the latter often providing the funds for services delivered by state and local units.

Public confidence in activist government was sustained at a high level during this period. Where FDR's New Deal innovations had extended the role of the federal government to provide for exigent human needs, Johnson's Great Society called upon Washington to vindicate the rights of sections of the American nation that had been denied equal rights, notably racial and ethnic minorities and women, and, subsequently, the handicapped and homosexuals.[15] Presidents were looked to for initiatives, while a more conservative Congress acted frequently to limit, restrain, even curb these initiatives. An example of the latter was Congress' rejection of President Truman's proposals for national health insurance. Activist government, with its emphasis on social responsibility, energized and expanded the activities of voluntary agencies and civic associations and of state and local governments, especially in the several areas of human services. The quarter century following World War II witnessed simultaneously a period of unparalleled economic prosperity and activist government.

The Conservative Restoration, 1969–Present

Anti-government reaction came to the fore during the Republican national convention of 1964, which signaled the capture of that party by its rejuvenated, militantly conservative Goldwater wing based in the

South and Southwest (the Sun Belt), areas that were growing at a faster rate, economically and demographically, than the rest of the country. This shift was financed by a new generation of self-made entrepreneurs who were militant apostles of laissez-faire and were hostile to government, taxes, and labor unions. The Democratic primaries of 1968 demonstrated a sharp white working-class backlash against federally sponsored civil rights and affirmative action programs that appeared to threaten their jobs and their neighborhoods, and reflected their disgust with the trashing of patriotism and traditional morality unleashed by resistance to the Vietnam War and the countercultural sex revolution of the mid-1960s. Disillusionment with government gained new converts with the youth rebellion against the Vietnam War, compounded by the Watergate scandal. Thus the traditional rightist antigovernment ranks were swollen by converts from the left.

The oil embargo of 1973 brought an abrupt end to the long period of post–World War II economic expansion and prosperity. Stagnant earnings followed shortly thereafter by double-digit inflation precipitated a taxpayers' revolt. There was a growing sense that reducing the tax burden and the scope of government might be more important than maintaining services. Thus, the time had come to rein in government waste, especially spending on "welfare," which was believed (falsely) to be a large component of the federal budget and to be distributed overgenerously to lazy and frequently immoral women ("welfare queens"). Under a conservative Democratic president, Jimmy Carter, mainline economists identified with the Democratic Party sponsored the deregulation of airlines, railways, telecommunications, radio and television, and electric power, without significant opposition from liberal and left-leaning intellectuals or politicians, signifying their loss of confidence in state-centered approaches to public policy. The late 1970s witnessed the maturing and the achievement of intellectual respectability for ideologically rightist journals and think tanks that had been initiated a generation before by a small band of wealthy enemies of activist government.[16] Student conservatism emerged for the first time as a prominent presence on university campuses.

These various streams of disenchantment with government were skillfully elaborated by Ronald Reagan in his successful 1980 presidential campaign. Vigorously exploiting the traditional cultural theme of suspicion of public authority, invoking laissez-faire ideology, preaching traditional morality, and cultivating the interests of corporate America,

Reagan and his associates aimed expressly to roll back the New Deal and Great Society programs and restore the minimal government state of the 1920s. (Reagan's political hero was, after all, Calvin Coolidge!) The emphasis on self-serving individualism and the diminished role of government were accompanied by the shrinking presence of civic voluntary associations, with private concerns supplanting social responsibility as the dominant ethos of the period. Reagan and his successor, George Bush, actively promoted an anti-government ideology intended to discredit all government interventions in the nation's economic and social affairs, except for the military, which was vastly expanded in order to wage the Cold War. Growing suspicion of foreigners in Republican ranks prompted a retreat from international cooperation and a reversion to militant unilateralism in foreign affairs. Taxes were drastically reduced, especially for corporations and high-income taxpayers, and it was made clear that the federal government would not be available for fresh initiatives.

Federal programs that could not be terminated or privatized were, where possible, to be devolved to state governments. The process of deregulation was to be accelerated. Appointments to the federal courts were subjected to an ideological litmus test to ensure their fidelity to "conservative" principles of judicial interpretation. The ideological tone that they set was promoted and reenforced by an aggressive and lavishly financed campaign by right-wing publicists to glorify market processes and discredit government and bureaucrats, identifying them with incompetence, corruption, massive waste, and threats to individual liberty. "Liberal" became a term of opprobrium, implying high taxes, wasteful expenditures, especially on welfare and foreign aid, the promotion of harebrained social experiments, loose sexual practices, and, for some, softness on communism and the sponsorship of godless "secular humanism."

The success of this ideological pressure undermined the Democrats' confidence in their orientation to public policy. The center of gravity shifted sharply to the right as the agenda of public policy reflected rightist values. Bill Clinton, a moderate Democrat committed to market economics, was elected to the presidency in 1992 in protest against President Bush's apparent lack of concern and inability to deal with the economic recession of the early 1990s. After failing to deliver on his campaign pledge to provide universal health protection, Clinton cautiously avoided new initiatives, adopted some Republican measures that cut back government programs (e.g., welfare and balanced budgets) while defending civil rights, the choice option for abortions, and resisting some of the more draconian proposals of the reactionary Republican majority that won a decisive victory in the congressional elections of 1994.

As the century draws to a close, the dominant public mood accepts Clinton's pronouncement that the era of big government is over. The burden of proof is on those who propose fresh government initiatives. At the same time, efforts to cut back popular middle-class programs, such as Social Security, Medicare, environmental protection, and the exemption from Federal income taxation of interest on home mortgages are resisted. Demonstrating their commitment to market capitalism, congressional Republicans are attempting to capitalize on the anti-government mood by campaigning to marketize Social Security and Medicare by creating individual retirement accounts that would be invested by their owners, and to privatize public education by issuing vouchers that would enable parents to use government funds to send their children to private schools.

The end of the Cold War, the modest prosperity of the Clinton era, and the welcome diminution in the incidence of violent crime have diminished the perception of need for activist government, while the campaign finance scandals associated with the 1996 elections and the impeachment of President Clinton have reenforced prevailing cynicism about politicians and government. Despite internal tensions on moral issues, a common anti-government ideology unites the several components of the current Republican-rightist coalition. They invest in and use the Republican Party as their common political vehicle. The components of the Democratic coalition have no such common vision; they invest only sporadically in the party and use it only guardedly to promote their separate interests. Instead of the Republicans' programmatic and strategic orientation, Democrats seem satisfied mainly to win elections, cling to office, and use their narrow victories to defend earlier accomplishments.

Shifting National Moods

Two centuries of experience demonstrate the rough periodization of dominant moods regarding the appropriate role of government in

American life. What the dominant mood determines is the relative ease or difficulty in placing on the national political agenda proposals that draw on the powers and resources of government to address what are believed to be national problems. Federally mandated consumer protection and resource conservation were summarily dismissed as unwarranted interference with property rights and states' rights during the laissez-faire/robber baron era, but with a sharp change in the dominant national mood, both were enacted by Progressives. During the FDR years, labor organization was encouraged and the national Labor Relations Act was implemented to protect labor unions; no such measure could have been contemplated during the anti-government mood of the Roaring Twenties. The Bank of the United States was established during the Federalist era, but no such expansion of government activities could have been considered during the Jacksonian era of minimal government.

The dominant mood reflects the distribution of political power, but how the political victors at any time decide to employ their power depends on the ideas that motivate them and justify their power. These ideas become hegemonic for a period of time, meaning that they establish the framework to which proposals must conform if they are to find their way to the public agenda. Nevertheless, initiatives once implemented may survive less friendly times if, like Social Security and environmental protection during the current era, they develop strong organized electoral constituencies whose political spokespersons are prepared to engage in rear-guard efforts to defend them.

This periodization is a good predictor of the prevailing tone of public policy, although it is never the whole story, because American politics has always been highly pluralistic. Minor currents may prevail, even when they are inconsistent with the trend of the times. Determined constituencies or inflamed public sentiment may secure government support for fresh initiatives during periods of passive government. For example, the Mexican War was fought during the era of minimal government prior to the Civil War; the Hawley-Smoot Act raised protective tariffs at the height of the anti-government, Roaring Twenties era; and while abruptly terminating Johnson's anti-poverty program, President Nixon felt constrained to expand federally enforced environmental protection. During peak periods of activist government, there has never been a threat to private ownership and operation of the means of production. Contrary to European experience, no significant sector of the economy was developed or taken over by government. Instead, the emphasis has been on directing the resources of the federal government to facilitate and serve the private economy, as was the case with the post–Civil War land grant subsidies to railroad developers and the post–World War II decision to draw on private enterprise for the peaceful development of atomic power.

Institutionally, periods of activist government are accompanied by enhancement of the powers of the presidency, while the powers of Congress expand and those of the president shrink during periods of relative passivity.[17] Given the structural diffusion of power in the U.S. government, the mobilization of opinion and of political support for fresh initiatives requires action from the sole source of effective national leadership. In the absence of presidential leadership, government initiative is difficult, because Congress lacks the capacity to focus the numerous diverse and competing interests it represents. When the dominant mood favors passive government, when there are few demands on the federal government to deal with exigent problems, presidents lack either the desire or the capacity to sponsor initiatives that expand the role of government. Congress then enters that vacuum with measures that cater to separate constituencies or enhance the power of its leading members. Woodrow Wilson's celebrated treatise, *Congressional Government*, describes the commanding role of Congress both at policy and administrative levels during the robber baron era of passive government at the close of the nineteenth century.[18]

Because suspicion of public authority is deeply ingrained in American culture, the ideology of limited government power has been the historic norm. Even when individuals and groups strongly advocate and defend particular programs that reflect their beliefs and interests, they retain a general doctrinal commitment to the principles of limited government, low taxes, and preference for state and local over federal initiatives—until crisis compels them to turn to Washington.[19] The burden of proof is on proposals to utilize federal resources and authority rather than those of states and localities. This enduring ideology, combined with genuine failings in the performance of the federal government and federal-level politicians, provided the raw material that was successfully exploited by committed enemies of activist government to create the cynicism of the 1980s and 1990s. Periods of national crisis resulting from war and the threat of war, economic depression, or the accumulation of neglected needs result in demands for government initiatives and create a mood that favors activist government even after the immediate crisis has passed. Activist programs in turn eventually generate controversies, create enemies, and spawn abuses that begin to discredit government action. When these dissatisfactions accumulate and combine with periods of prosperity and general satisfaction with the status quo, skeptics and opponents of activist government, whatever their motives, successfully invoke the powerful cultural theme of suspicion of public authority. A new mood becomes dominant, partisans of activist government become disheartened and marginalized, a new era of passive government ensues, renewing the cycle that has characterized American experience with government.

A Caution

When in this and later chapters, I refer to the Republican-rightist position on issues of public policy, I recognize that the Republican Party, like all major parties in American politics, is a catch-all organization. It includes on its margins a contingent of "moderates" or pragmatists based mainly in the Northeast, who, in the Eisenhower-Rockefeller tradition, are tolerant on social issues such as abortion and homosexuality and accept the need for some government action to deal with social and economic problems that cannot be adequately managed by market processes. Included in the moderate camp are Republican governors whose executive functions are believed to require them to take a more pragmatic view of public policy. Among them, George W. Bush, the likely Republican 2000 presidential nominee, is considered to be a moderate.

Nevertheless, the central tendency of the national party, beginning in the Reagan era and as exemplified by its current congressional leadership, is firmly attached to the anti-government, laissez-faire, states' rights ideology (chapter 2) and strongly influenced by the moral outlook of their evangelical component. When I speak of the Republican right, it is this dominant core of the party that I have in mind. I understand that the party includes among its active politicians and officeholders a minority of moderates and pragmatists who do not adhere to some of the positions espoused by those who now control the party machinery and speak and legislate in its name.

CHAPTER FOUR

An Activist Government
for Twenty-First-Century America

We, the people of the United States, in order to form a more perfect
union, establish justice, insure domestic tranquillity, provide for the
common defense, promote the general welfare and insure the blessings of liberty for ourselves and our posterity do ordain and establish this Constitution for the United States of America.

—Preamble to the Constitution

How Long Will This Cycle Last?

I predict a limited shelf life for the Republican-rightist anti-government
crusade, despite its resonance with an important continuing strain of
popular culture. The simple reason is that the goals outlined by the
Founders—a more perfect union, the common defense, the general
welfare, the blessings of liberty—cannot under contemporary conditions be realized by minimalist government, market processes, and the
separate, uncoordinated activities of fifty states. Indeed, the Founding
Fathers believed they were establishing institutions and providing
powers for a government whose activities would be limited in the interest of preserving liberty yet would be adequate to the challenges of
their era and flexible enough to accommodate the changing needs of
posterity. The rightist nostalgia for the supposed golden age that preceded the Great Depression of the 1930s, exacerbated as that disaster
was by a neglectful and unresponsive federal government, takes no account of the contemporary integrated economy and information networks dominated by a handful of giant multinational corporations and
financial houses, of the insecurities produced by a competitive and
rapidly evolving economy in a highly urbanized society, or of the
global interests and responsibilities of the United States as the paramount world power. Indeed, the most conspicuous contradiction in
their minimalist program is its exemption of the armed forces, whose

57

financing, equipping, and management presuppose a large and active federal government.

At the political level, this project is bound to fall apart under the stress of competing goals and competing interests. The most conspicuous is the Republicans' chronic and passionate temptation to cut taxes—their electoral trump card—versus their latter-day commitment to fiscal austerity and balanced budgets. The conflict between deficit hawks and tax cutters fatally confused the message of their 1996 presidential campaign. As prosperity and President Clinton's espousal of balanced budgets preempted the former theme, their emphasis shifted to tax cutting, notably the campaign to eliminate the progressive income tax under the guise of simplifying the federal tax code. The budget surpluses that were unexpectedly realized in 1998 and are projected to accelerate well into the twenty-first century presuppose the maintenance of late 1990s prosperity. While prosperity continues, tax cutting must compete with goals such as financially fortifying Social Security and Medicare (which Republicans have difficulty resisting), drawing down the national debt, strengthening public education, and incremental improvements in health coverage for vulnerable segments of the population, such as children and the near-elderly. And if the cycle of the 1990s economic expansion should be succeeded by recession, then all bets are off, for federal revenues would contract just as expenditures to relieve unemployment and stimulate recovery would sharply increase. In that event, Republican deficit hawks would feel compelled to block further tax reductions.

Middle-class anxieties and insecurities culminating in the anger that triggered the 1994 rejection of the Democrats are not addressed in rightist doctrine. Uncertainties about health care, employment security, and affordable college tuitions cannot be alleviated by market processes. Republicans' failure to propose any measures to relieve these uncertainties leaves them vulnerable to rejection by middle-class and working-class voters as callous, uncaring, and unconcerned with the lot of the average working family. The moderate wing of the Republican Party, though marginalized in recent years, would break ranks and join with Democrats in supporting such measures, as well as proposals to strengthen environmental protection.

If public services should be further reduced, their quality and reliability will deteriorate. The effects will be felt in declining levels of environmental protection; in neglect of the transportation infrastructure, including airline and highway safety; in higher costs for student loans in the face of increased tuitions; in weak enforcement of labor standards, consumer protection, and immigration laws; and in inconvenience to the public.[1] Inadequate inspection of meat products and imported fruits and vegetables has been responsible for widespread illnesses in recent years and heightened public concern over the security of the nation's food supply. Neglected maintenance of national parks in the face of record-breaking visits has already caused breakdowns in their infrastructure, threatening very heavy capital expenditures at Yellowstone, Yosemite, and Grand Canyon if these national treasures are to be preserved. Sharp staff reduction in the Internal Revenue Service plus rightist attacks on its collection methods have resulted in tens of billions of dollars in overdue but unpaid revenue owed to the federal government in income taxes. Many of these obligations will be successfully evaded by the depleted IRS's inability to collect these taxes.

The notorious prevalence of sweatshops in the garment industry is evidence of the current inability of the federal government to enforce its labor laws. These shortcomings will begin to mobilize angry middle-class constituencies in favor of improved financing and even expansion rather than reduction or termination of public services. The majority of Americans favor and believe they benefit from specific public services, which explains why they were initiated in the first place.

The rightist coalition harbors other cleavages that will test its survivability as its factions demand that it deliver on election promises. Many of the advocates of limited government / low taxes / supply-side economics are social libertarians. Tolerant of women's freedom of reproductive choice and of homosexual rights, they favor the continued separation of church and state, and oppose government censorship of the arts and the media. The evangelical right, which provides essential grassroots support for the rightist coalition, insists that tangible action be taken on behalf of their demands. While they support lower taxes and minimal government on economic matters, they demand government espousal and enforcement of their moral agenda. They have grown impatient of symbolic support by the Republican leadership on such issues as abortion, homosexuality, school prayer, and government financing of private schools.

Within that coalition are tensions between true believers and pragmatists. The former would drive ahead with all elements of the rightist agenda, such as the impeachment of President Clinton, even if this should spell electoral setbacks; the latter would trim their sails to avoid defeat. How long this coalition can hold together without defections is anybody's guess. These vulnerabilities are enhanced as components of their electoral support base decide, as they did in the 1996 presidential race, that other concerns, for example, protection of Medicare, low-cost student loans, environmental services, or an attractive candidate, are more salient to their interests.

But the coming disenchantment with this anti-government message and the unraveling of the rightist coalition will not necessarily displace Republicans or improve the fortunes of Democrats and progressives unless the latter can produce a feasible and persuasive alternative ideology and program. None has yet emerged. Warmed-over rightist themes (balanced budgets, welfare reform, unrestricted free trade, and smaller, "reinvented" government), like those advocated by some of President Clinton's associates, fall far short of a persuasive alternative vision that might inspire a political movement. Central to such a vision must be an unapologetic acceptance of a positive role for government, especially of the federal government, in meeting the needs of American society, many of which have been neglected or ignored during the past quarter century. It should emphasize that a strong and active federal government does not imply weaker state and local government or weaker community initiatives through non-governmental voluntary service and charitable organizations (NGOs). An activist federal government provides resources and incentives that stimulate action by states, localities, and citizen associations. This was demonstrated conclusively during the era of the Great Society. In the wake of the Great Society programs, many state and local governments finally modernized their structures and expanded their capabilities better to serve their citizens, while voluntary agencies, an important component of civil society, became more active than at any previous time. Rightist solicitude for state government and for the Tenth Amendment conceals their real ideological objective, which is to weaken and disable government at all levels.

Criteria for Allocating Responsibilities

Article 1 of the Constitution confers certain powers on the federal government. Powers not so conferred or reasonably implied from them or necessary and proper to their execution are reserved to the states and the people by the Tenth Amendment. Certain federal functions, such as the war power, the treaty power, and the power to issue currency and borrow on the credit of the United States, are exclusive and cannot be exercised by the states. Others, such as the regulation of interstate commerce and the levying and collection of taxes are discretionary; in the absence of federal action they may be exercised by the states. But once the United States has exercised such powers, the states are preempted under the supremacy clause of Article VI. The states may, however, act in ways that complement but do not interfere with federal operations.

Congress has considerable discretion in applying federal powers and in making laws that are necessary and proper to implement the enumerated powers. In the exercise of its power to raise and support armies and to provide and maintain a navy, Congress may choose to establish and operate government-owned arsenals, factories, and shipyards to produce and repair weapons and matériel; or it may decide to purchase goods and services from private producers. Changes in circumstances, such as the integration of the American economy, may induce Congress and the courts to reinterpret the scope of federal powers. For example, the regulation of interstate and foreign commerce has gradually incorporated the production and marketing of virtually all commodities as well as labor relations and labor standards, since virtually all goods and services now move across state lines. The power to lay and collect taxes to provide for the general welfare depends on the judges' understanding of what is included in the concept of general welfare.

Where reasonable people differ is over the scope of these discretionary powers. "Conservatives," including most current members of the Republican right, prefer to limit the range of federal action on social and economic matters; "liberals" and progressives tend to interpret the language of the Constitution more broadly, as authorizing federal action whenever constitutional language can be construed as applying to contemporary conditions. Both sides agree that federal powers are limited by numerous constitutional provisions, including those guaranteeing individual liberties and requiring due process and equal protection of the laws.

Over the years, as statesmen, judges, and scholars have debated the proper range of discretionary federal powers, two general criteria have emerged. Like the language of the Constitution itself, these may be interpreted narrowly or broadly, depending on individual outlooks. These alternative interpretations are taken up by and reflect the competitive preferences of economic, social, ideological, and regional interest groups and thus become the substance of politics and political debate. Business interests and their Republican supporters tend to interpret these criteria narrowly, preferring allocation by market processes or by the states; labor, environmentalists, minorities, and those identified as Democrats take a more expansive view of the range of permissible federal action. Yet, two criteria for determining the optimal assignment of activities to the federal government, state governments, local authorities, voluntary associations, or the private, for-profit (market) sector are widely accepted as reasonable and have stood the test of time:

1. Is the proposed activity of substantive importance to the security, health, well-being, or convenience of society, to economic stability and prosperity, or to the defense and promotion of basic rights? If not, it is no concern of government.
2. Where is the principal competence or potential capacity for performing each activity? Some activities, of course, are more productively shared by networks that draw on the capabilities of several of these institutions.

Despite rightist rhetoric that ambitious federal politicians and bureaucrats, prompted by "interest groups," have, since the era of the New Deal, reached out through taxation, regulation, and spending to usurp activities from the states or markets, the very opposite has been the case. The federal government has assumed functions only when states and the private sector have proved unable or unwilling to undertake them. Neither party has, during this century, challenged a fundamental premise of American economic culture: that the production and distribution of marketable goods and services should be the province of private enterprise. Even as security sensitive a field as nuclear energy and the actual manufacturing of nuclear weapons have been entrusted from the outset, beginning with the Truman administration, to private enterprise.

The bicameral structure of Congress, the lengthy committee hearings, and the public debate that precedes every new initiative guarantee that new responsibilities will be undertaken by federal authority only when other possibilities are unavailable. The federal government took over the operation of the eastern freight and passenger rail services (Conrail and Amtrak) only after their private owners had abandoned these essential services. The federal role in environmental regulation became inevitable as citizen pressures impressed the issue of air and water pollution on the public agenda, while corporate and local government polluters declined to limit their emissions voluntarily and the fifty state governments proved unable or unwilling to cope with a problem that had become regional and national in scale.

This chapter specifies a set of activities that are essential to the well-being of the American nation as it confronts the third millenium and are appropriate for administration by the federal government. Each of these activities is consistent with the dual criteria outlined in this chapter— substantive necessity and principal competence. These activities include conducting an "energetic" foreign policy; managing the national economy in the face of globalizing pressures in order to balance the goals of price stability, economic growth, and full employment; providing essential public services that are beyond the capacities of private enterprise and state and local governments; exercising the countervailing power that protects the public interest and the more vulnerable sections of society from abusive concentrations of economic power; and safeguarding the institutions of the American political system.

Essential Functions of the Federal Government

An Energetic Foreign Policy

The *Federalist Papers* demonstrate that to Hamilton and other Founders, a paramount purpose of the new Republic was to provide government with the means to conduct an active foreign policy, one that promotes and defends U.S. security and economic stakes, while embracing the concept of enlightened self-interest.[2] Enlightened self-interest requires the United States to be fully engaged in world affairs, to contribute along with other nations and in the spirit of give and take to international agreements that promote global and regional security, economic expansion, environmental safety, the relief of suffering, and the alleviation of Third World poverty. Only within the framework of enlightened self-interest and in cooperation with other states and with international organizations including the United Nations, can the United States effectively pursue its specific foreign-policy goals: to safeguard global sources of supply; promote overseas market opportunities for goods, services, and investments; deter and punish enemies, including terrorist organizations; defend friendly regimes; and promote human rights and democratic development.

As the world's unchallenged military and economic superpower, the American people should enjoy a sense of security sufficient to provide leadership for peaceful and orderly world development. Unless the United States is prepared to engage constructively with other nations and be sensitive to their interests, the latter will not respect our leadership or be receptive to accommodate our interests and preferences. Yet, in the absence of our leadership, the international order that we seek cannot be sustained. A number of the goals that we seek for ourselves cannot be accomplished except in cooperation with other states. The pursuit of these goals requires an active diplomacy, a willingness to work with like-minded nations and contribute a fair share of manpower and financing to common purposes. It also requires a robust, excellently equipped, well-trained, combat-ready military establishment tailored to the needs of the post–Cold War world, and a willingness to deploy these forces to trouble spots in coordination, where possible, with other nations.

It seems strange that fifty years after World War II and after the successes of the Marshall Plan and NATO, it should be necessary to argue against narrow nationalism and a reversion to xenophobia, isolationism, and unilateralism in an era of instant global communications and unprecedented economic integration. The current rightist posture toward foreigners is as suspicious, cynical, and mean-spirited as their attitude toward the poor and minorities in this country. Recent examples have been their sneering and defiant attitude toward the very moderate global warming agreement hammered out in Kyoto, their unwillingness to honor our large debt to the United Nations, their rejection of the comprehensive Nuclear Test Ban Treaty, and their opposition to U.S. participation in the NATO campaign against ethnic cleansing in Kosovo.[3] Though many Congressional Republicans accept America's international leadership responsibilities and reject the neo-isolationist label, they have surrendered legislative initiative to unilateralists and supported them on critical votes. Neo-isolationism is attenuated in Republican-rightist circles mainly by the commitment of its corporate constituency to export promotion and free trade as a federal responsibility.

There are two expressions of neo-isolationism abroad in the United States. The first and most consequential is the current rightist version, whose most prominent apostles are Pat Buchanan and Jesse Helms. Similar attitudes found their way into mainstream Republican doctrine and rhetoric with the rightists' 1994 "Contract with America." They appear to regard the United Nations as an evil conspiracy of devious foreigners and parasitical functionaries, hostile to American interests and values, and bent on making the United States waste its funds on multilateralist and socialistic schemes of no benefit to this country. Their proposal to subtract the U.S. financial contribution to peacekeeping operations from the annual U.S. contributions to the UN would effectively eliminate the UN peacekeeping function.

Recognizing that the United States cannot withdraw entirely from world affairs, rightists are prepared to engage with others but only on our terms. Contrary to the unilateralists, however, the United States cannot take care of all our objectives on our own—avoiding global economic depression, preventing epidemics, controlling nuclear proliferation and the drug traffic, combating terrorism, or promoting human rights.[4] Other nations will not cooperate with us unless we are prepared to take their interests into account. Despite our overwhelming military superiority, our people are not prepared to pay the price in lives and treasure to impose our will on others by military intervention, as have the great empires in world history, even if this were possible. We must win their support by persuasion, bargaining, and occasionally compromise. Thus, unilateralism is dangerously misguided. Progressives recognize that in some situations we have no alternative but to act on our own; normally, however, as an expression of our enlightened self-interest, we must engage our considerable influence with other states in the spirit of give and take.

The less influential leftist isolationism is a legacy of the Vietnam experience and the tendency of the United States during the Cold War to support corrupt and repressive regimes in Third World countries on anti-communist grounds. It is premised on the view that the United States acts as the principal agent of global capitalist-imperialist exploitation and repression of popular forces that can best be counteracted by ceasing to interfere in the affairs of other countries. These rightist-leftist expressions of isolationism are mutually reenforcing, reaching similar conclusions from opposite extremes, both destructive of America's enlightened self-interest in an interdependent world.

A word on immigration policy. Uncontrolled, illegal immigration on a massive scale is an abuse that most Americans are no longer willing to tolerate. Beginning in the 1970s, neither party has been willing to address this problem forthrightly, Democrats because of the opposition of civil libertarians and the organized Hispanic communities, Republicans because immigration lowers labor costs for influential employer constituencies and contributes to the weakening of labor unions. The effects of illegal immigration on so large a scale—an estimated 6 million—is to bring our laws into contempt, poison the political environment for legal resident aliens, inflate the costs of state governments, lower wage levels for unskilled workers, and increase the number of children being raised in poverty. The time has come to begin to enforce our immigration laws, which remain the world's most liberal: between 1961 and 1995, our doors were opened to more than 20 million legal immigrants, at an annual rate of 582,000. (For 1995, that figure reached 720,000.) [5] Most Americans recognize the contributions that successive waves of immigration have added to America's strength and quality of life; they would continue to welcome immigration in compliance with our laws and persevere in our compassionate policy toward genuine victims of religious and political oppression.[6]

While immigration is changing the racial and ethnic proportions in our population, the goal of immigration policy must remain the pursuit of an integrated and inclusive American national community bound together by a common set of values, aspirations, and institutions that comprise the American secular creed. This community communicates in a common medium, the English language.[7] This goal would be subverted by the cultivation of segregated identity enclaves, as advocated by the current trendy doctrine of "multiculturalism." As they have throughout American history, members of ethnic communities, while integrating into American society, would remain free to preserve and develop their inherited cultures on a voluntary basis.

Protective and Countervailing Power

The great strength of capitalism and of market economics is its drive for efficiency, innovation, and expansion resulting from the incentives of competitive profit seeking. Its principal problems are its tendency toward monopoly, against which Adam Smith warned two centuries ago, its preoccupation with short-term results, and its disregard for so-cietal interests and for those who are less able to or less successful in coping with competitive market processes. Under unregulated market competition, there is a structural tendency for productive capacity to outstrip demand. To continue to prosper and even to survive, owners and managers seek to restrain the costs of production, a principal com-ponent of which is labor. Unless this drive to reduce labor costs can be curtailed by some countervailing force, labor's share in increasing pro-ductivity is likely to fall. Labor will not share equitably in productiv-ity growth, and wages will stagnate or even fall in real terms, as they did in the United States in the two decades following the late 1970s; the benefits will flow disproportionately in profits and executive com-pensation to owners and managers. The failure of wages to advance at the same rate as productivity growth contributes, in turn, to shortfalls in aggregate demand that precipitates economic depressions.[8]

There are two major expressions of countervailing power: collective action, for example, by labor unions and consumer societies, and gov-ernment action, in the form of minimum wages, the earned-income tax credit, farm price supports, and such public services as Social Security, Medicare, and Medicaid, which redistribute income from taxpayers to the beneficiaries of those services. Labor unions have been greatly weakened during the past two decades, while laissez-faire and anti-government pressures have limited the role of government.

Recognition of this need for countervailing power became the cen-terpiece of European social democracy, Catholic humanist doctrine, and the American Progressive movement a century ago, with its stric-tures against the abuses of unregulated capitalism; its attacks on the "trusts" (monopolies) and on concentrated economic power ("male-factors of great wealth"); its sponsorship of the conservation move-ment; its support of legislation in favor of workmen's compensation, the eight-hour day, and the protection of working women and children; and its identification of a public interest that transcends those of par-ticular industries, regions, or constituencies. The need for federal ac-tion to provide countervailing power, protect the public interest, and check abuses against the more vulnerable sections of society was en-dorsed by the two presidents produced by the Progressive movement, Republican Theodore Roosevelt and Democrat Woodrow Wilson.

Under the New Deal of the 1930s, these responsibilities of the fed-eral government were exemplified in such measures as the Home Owners Loan Act, to protect home owners from massive foreclosures of mortgages by banks and insurance companies; the Securities and Exchange Act, to protect investors from fraudulent and deceptive manipulation on Wall Street; the National Labor Relations Act, to secure the rights of labor unions to organize and bargain collectively; the Agricultural Adjustment Act, to put a floor under farm prices; the Fair Labor Standards Act, which outlawed child labor and mandated minimum wages and maximum hours of work; the Federal Deposit Insurance Corporation, to protect depositors from bank failures; and the reinvigoration of the Federal Trade Commission and the anti-trust division of the Justice Department, after a moribund period during previous administrations.

The Great Society of the 1960s expanded protective activities ranging from the safety of food products and pharmaceuticals; to protecting consumers from false and deceptive advertising; occupational health, safety, and sanitation practices in the workplace; safeguarding the civil rights of minorities and women; and environmental protection, which is now supported by large and vigorous public constituencies.

With some notable exceptions, organized business interests, which finance the Republican Party, and their spokespersons are lukewarm or actively hostile to this pattern of countervailing regulation. They complain that federal regulation imposes onerous, costly, intrusive, and needless burdens on business, that the necessary control of abuses could be provided by market competition, fiscal incentives, state governments, or voluntary self-regulation. Hostility to regulation and to the protective function of the federal government have been incorporated into the current rightist ideology. The 1994 Contract with America included a moratorium on federal regulatory activity until the Republican Congress could decide which of them to reduce or terminate, plus a requirement that economic benefit–cost analysis be applied to all regulations, including those that deal with health and safety, and that affected property owners be fully compensated for the financial consequences of environmental regulations. The Reagan and Bush administrations attempted to hobble many of the federal regulatory agencies by limiting their funding, appointing administrators who were unfriendly to their mandate, and creating an atmosphere that was hostile to regulation; Democratic Congresses were able to spare these activities from drastic impairment. In the event, the enforcement of many of these protective measures has become weak and ineffective. One of the most conspicuous examples is the aforementioned flourishing of nineteenth-century sweatshops in defiance of the wage and hours provisions of the Fair Labor Standards Act and the safety standards mandated by the Occupational Health and Safety Act.

In an integrated and globalized economy such as ours, only the federal government is equipped to check abuses of concentrated economic power; to protect unorganized consumers, investors, depositors, and workers; and to safeguard the environment and our patrimony of natural resources. Fifty state governments are capable of action in support of federal initiatives and of limited measures such as building codes and the protection of water supply, but they are often disabled by the pressures of locally based economic interests and by the prevailing mobility of capital as the states compete with one another to attract investments by creating more favorable (e.g., low taxes, regulation free, "right to work") climates for business operations—in a race to the bottom.

The United States has become economically and culturally "one nation, indivisible." The abuses of concentrated economic power and of unregulated business practices are national in scope, with national consequences that can be dealt with only by regulation that is national in coverage. Indeed, more and more problems such as environmental protection have become transnational in scope, requiring diplomatic negotiation and action by international treaties or multinational organizations. The claim espoused by true believers in the rightist ideology—that these problems can be dealt with by fifty state governments—is, in effect, a campaign to eliminate such regulations altogether. In some forms of regulation, such as highway safety and nursing home standards, it is possible and even desirable to combine uniform federal standards with flexible implementation and enforcement by state governments.

The claim that business can practice self-regulation, setting and enforcing voluntary standards among the members of particular industries, is indeed fanciful. Though many corporations, including some of the largest, would contribute to shaping such standards and faithfully adhere to them, there is conclusive evidence that many would not. The savings and loan debacle, criminal behavior on Wall Street, widespread fraud in defense contracting, large-scale fraud and abuses of patients by health maintenance organizations and insurance companies, violations of safety standards by commercial airlines, the aforementioned sweatshops, and the efforts by tobacco companies to induce teenagers to smoke demonstrate that there are always some firms, large and small, that in pursuit of expanded markets and higher profits are prepared to cut corners and engage in sharp practices that victimize the public, even when they knowingly and patently violate the law.[9] How much more prone would they be to indulge in such practices in a risk-free environment of "self-regulation"! Indeed, many reputable business leaders, contrary to paid spokespersons for organized business associations, argue that legitimate business needs the protection of some federal regulations. In this vein, leading pharmaceutical manufacturers argue that the regulatory activities of the Food and Drug Administration must be preserved from zealots in Congress in order to protect legitimate manufacturers and sustain global confidence in the integrity of U.S. pharmaceutical products.

Contrary to the litany of rightist propaganda, federal regulations are seldom the product of power-hungry federal bureaucrats. Though this allegation, in the absence of effective counterargument by Democratic politicians and spokespersons for the moderate left, has achieved the status of conventional wisdom, it is seldom sustained by evidence. Most legislation authorizing regulation and the administrative implementation that follow are consequences of scandals and serious problems that journalists and important constituencies bring to the attention of government, for example, the pollution of air and water, automotive safety, insider manipulation on Wall Street, breakdowns in financial institutions, the marketing of dangerous drugs and contaminated foods, or unsanitary and hazardous working conditions. Before regulations are enacted, public hearings are held. There is continual scrutiny by congressional committees, and aggrieved parties have the right of appeal to the courts.

Business interests that believe they are unfairly penalized by proposed regulations, for example, the automobile industry's original opposition to safety, fuel efficiency, and anti-pollution measures (replicated currently in similar opposition to global warming standards), are well endowed with the political muscle to express their views. The procedures are anything but arbitrary. That some regulations and proposed regulations are ill advised, excessive, obsolete, cumbersome, and overzealous is inevitable, but such specific measures may and should be challenged in many forums and revised or eliminated. This is a far cry from the current campaign to dismantle the entire federal function of providing a protective and countervailing force for American society.[10]

Government functions either through the services it provides, as outlined in this chapter, or through regulation. Its regulatory activities are always contentious. Regulations that were needed at one point in history may become outdated and inhibit beneficial progress, as occurred in the transportation industry prior to the deregulation of airlines, highway traffic, and railroads in the late 1970s. On the other hand, some industries may be committing such widespread abuses of the public interest as to require not less, but more rigorous regulation, a prime example being the health maintenance organizations and their associated insurance companies during the 1990s. Since the need for specific regulations evolve over time, all regulatory regimes need to be monitored and modified to ensure that, as far as possible, they are providing optimal regulation, balancing the public interest with opportunities for technological progress and competitive efficiency.

It has become clear in recent years that where genuine competition is possible, market processes provide economically more efficient regulation than administrative processes. The latter are often cumbersome, ill-informed, and vulnerable to capture by regulated interests through political manipulation. In the absence of genuine competition, governments should first attempt to achieve the conditions for such competition by anti-monopoly and similar measures, but where these are unavailing, administrative regulation continues to be necessary in order to protect the public interest. Market processes, however, have proved of little value in protecting the public interest in safety, health, labor standards, environmental protection, equal opportunity, and similar non-economic areas where the role of government has expanded, despite the anti-regulatory pressures of the past two decades. Such experiments as providing for the marketization of pollution rights based on standards set by government may succeed in reducing the need for some administrative regulation, but they will not eliminate the necessity for vigorous government action to protect the welfare of unorganized members of the public.

In virtually every industry large-scale mergers are swelling the size of major corporations that now operate on a worldwide scale. The task of exercising public oversight—countervailing power—over these huge global conglomerates will challenge the regulatory capacities of governments. The problem will be complicated by the ability of these wealthy megacorporations to exert political pressure on members of Congress and the Executive Branch and to fight their battles in the courts. It will be necessary to innovate new methods of protecting the public interest under these new conditions, but this much is clear: in the absence of viable international institutions, only the federal government can command the political authority and the legal and administrative resources needed to apply effective countervailing power.

Providing Necessary Services

Here we refer to services that (a) are required by American society at its current stage of social and economic development, (b) cannot be provided at reasonable cost and effectiveness by private firms, (c) are beyond the competence of the fifty individual state governments, but (d) a compelling public interest requires that they be performed by a politically accountable agency. Unlike most of Europe, where important enterprises such as railways and telephone service have long been operated by the state, the U.S. economy is entirely in the hands of private firms, so that there is little scope for further privatization of industry. Privatization of public services such as prisons, libraries, and hospitals usually involves government financing and contract operations by profit-making firms. But privatization imposes significant contract-monitoring costs on government, with debatable consequences in terms of costs, quality, and reliability of services, or maintenance of labor standards.[11] Many federal activities have already (by 1998) been contracted out to private firms, thus reducing labor costs, because private firms tend to pay lower wages and provide smaller health and pension benefits than government agencies.

What I shall outline very briefly below are categories of public services that require federal action—an irreducible but not exhaustive listing. In some cases these services, financed by Washington and subject to federal standards, can be operated by states, local governments, or private firms and voluntary agencies, bringing local experience to bear on national problems and adapting federal standards to local conditions. Predictably, rightists oppose federal standards even when they involve federal funds provided to the states for the administration of specific programs; such was their reaction to President Clinton's proposal to provide federal funds to the states for day-care centers, despite numerous reports of child abuse and callous corruption by day-care providers presumably regulated by state agencies.

The first of these services is interstate transportation and communications, costly facilities that are vital to the mobility of citizens, the efficient movement of goods, and the operations of a competitive, integrated economy. The physical infrastructure of the economy includes the "Eisenhower" interstate highway system, major ports, harbors and airports, coastal and inland waterways, urban mass transit, and the airways, including the operation of the latter facilities and the vital supervision of airline safety.[12] There is little dispute that the nation's physical infrastructure must remain a responsibility of government. While telecommunications and Internet facilities and operations are in the hands of large profit-making firms, whose rates and practices are regulated by interfirm competition or by government agencies, governance of the radio-television spectrum, including policies affecting the operations of licensees, is the responsibility of the Federal Communications Commission. These facilities must continue to be supervised by a federal agency.

The second is the financing and promotion of scientific and technical research, including basic research in the major science disciplines and applied research for agriculture, industry, medicine, defense and space, and social behavior.[13] Unlike applied research conducted by private firms, where information becomes proprietary, most of this research is contracted to universities. Its findings are disseminated and made freely available to scientists, scholars, and other interested users anywhere in the world. Much of our leading international position in the physical and biological sciences, medicine, agricultural practices, military weaponry, space science, and many branches of engineering and industry can be traced directly to the output of these federally sponsored research activities to the point that even enthusiastic advocates of minimal government concede the need to continue large-scale federal support for the sciences.

There is widespread celebration of America's leading position in the new information technologies and in biotechnology, which have begun to transform many sectors of modern life—industrial production, distribution, communications, medicine, agriculture—and whose momentum will extend many decades into the future. The commercialization of these technologies promise substantial and sustained improvements in productivity and quality of life. America's leadership in the application and expansion of these technologies can be traced to the entrepreneurial climate in the economy and to the aforementioned sponsorship and generous funding of scientific research by the federal government since World War II. To sustain this leadership, the federal government must expand its support of basic research and the training of successive generations of scientists, take vigorous measures to prevent monopoly of commercial applications, incorporate these technologies into government's own operations, and strengthen public education, now the weakest link in this chain, so that the oncoming generation will be equipped to staff positions generated by these technologies.

To ensure that the benefits are equitably shared, government needs to facilitate the transition of people displaced by these technologies so that they do not become a neglected underclass. Government will also be called upon to exercise social control over technological applications, to protect public health, safety, welfare, and community values from their deleterious consequences. Though some technocratic enthusiasts urge government to step aside and entrust regulation to market processes in the global economy, government will continue to be required to regulate as well as to promote and facilitate the industries spawned by these revolutionary technologies. A foretaste of demands on the federal government to exercise social control over these technologies is the anti-monopoly action against Microsoft Corporation, the restrictions on human cloning, and limitations on inciting of violence on the Internet.

Related to the information function is the network of federal agencies that gather, analyze, and publish data that become authoritative and are essential to the shaping of policy and the functioning of a sophisticated, integrated economy. These agencies include the Weather Bureau, the Census Bureau, the Bureau of Labor Statistics, the Geological Survey, the Coast and Geodetic Survey, the Federal Reserve Board, and the Department of Agriculture through their statistical services.

Federal assistance to the sciences also includes support for university scholarships for advanced study in the natural, physical, and social sciences and in engineering. Such support ensures a supply of high-level expertise for our high-technology industries and sufficient instructors to train the oncoming generation of students. Scholarships for intensive study of foreign areas and languages are instrumental to our national security and economic interests. Fulbright awards for postgraduate research and study abroad and the Peace Corps program for service in low-income countries are successful federal initiatives that should be continued and expanded.

Third is the maintenance of basic protections for the elderly and the expansion of services for children, including such big-ticket entitlements as old age and survivors' insurance (Social Security) and medical and health care (Medicare) that enable the elderly to enjoy their declining years in dignity, with peace of mind and in relative security and comfort. Some gaps in these services need to be corrected, such as assisting seniors with the high costs of prescription drugs. Because these programs also contribute directly to the financial obligations of government, they need to be controlled and trimmed at the margin. This goal can be accomplished through various measures: adjusting cost-of-living increments to more accurately reflect their impact on senior citizens, gradually raising the age of eligibility, imposing tighter enforcement of billing practices by medical and health providers, and permitting managed health organizations to control costs by competitive bidding. Progressives must face up to the high costs of these popular entitlements, which are increasing annually at a much more rapid rate than economic growth. Democrats have been reluctant to address this problem, in part because of their concern that Republicans will attempt to use the resultant savings to further reduce tax rates for upper-income citizens, in effect transferring income from the elderly to the rich.[14]

Though logically incompatible with the ideology of radical individualism and minimal government, Republicans concede the political imperative of preserving these entitlements in some form. Republicans would, however, privatize them, where possible, by converting these entitlements' current universalistic insurance feature to individual accounts that would yield benefits commensurate with individual contributions and privately managed investments in the securities markets. Such a move would be a boon to the stock market and to brokerage firms but would greatly increase the risk to future annuitants of poor investment decisions and the volatility of securities markets, undermining the security provided by the current insurance arrangements. There may be merit in prudently investing, under the guidance of politically accountable experts, a portion of Social Security contributions in securities markets rather than in lower-yielding Treasury bonds, but not by breaking the system into individual privately managed accounts. Republicans reject this proposal, fearing the possible manipulation of shares in private sector firms by a government entity.

Though children represent the nation's future, the importance of their physical, intellectual, and moral development is not now reflected in public policy. We have been underinvesting in this most precious of our resources. The United States is the only industrialized nation that fails to mandate paid maternity leave for expectant mothers, or provide publicly financed and supervised day care for the children of working parents, or supply regular physical exams and medical care for children from low-income families. Children from families with up to 200 percent of poverty-level incomes should be eligible under federal grants-in-aid for Medicaid (health care for persons with sub-poverty level incomes), including hospitalization, physician coverage, immunizations, and preventive care. (This standard, currently the law in New York State, should be federalized by Congress and implemented with federal funds.)

The responsibilities of the federal government for public education (see the fifth point) must include initiatives to help the states reduce class size, improve the qualifications of teachers, and provide safe and attractive classrooms with modern teaching and learning equipment. Nutritional supplements (school lunch programs) and Head Start opportunities for children from deprived backgrounds must be maintained. After-school programs financed by Washington but operated by voluntary associations should be available to provide supervised recreation and enriched learning opportunities, especially for children of working parents and low-income families. Organized school-to-work opportunities should be available in cooperation with employers, equivalent to the European apprentice system, so that high school students who do not intend to go to college may be prepared for productive roles in our emergent high-technology economy.

Adequate investment in our children will help eliminate some of the consequences of the national scandal of 20–25 percent of children being brought up in poverty. These investments will not be cost-free, but they will salvage millions of youngsters from lives of crime, drug dependency, ill health, and poverty and provide them with the skills and the opportunity to function as responsible and productive citizens, workers, and family members.[15] The goals of national inclusiveness and equality of opportunity will remain hollow slogans as long as large numbers of children are condemned by accident of birth to face life with inferior education, inadequate nutrition and health care, and substandard housing. Although state governments and voluntary associations can contribute to the alleviation of this predicament, only the federal government can muster the resources and the leadership required to guarantee all our children a genuinely level playing field.

Fourth, and most controversial, are services that are national in scope though often local in impact and that seriously affect the health, welfare, security, and safety of large sections of the American public. These services include unemployment insurance; public health, including epidemiology; national health insurance; education and rehabilitation programs to combat the drug epidemic; urban redevelopment; disaster relief; reliable and affordable day care for low-income working parents; low-income housing; decent subsistence for the mentally and physically handicapped; and such measures as job training and aggressive placement services to assist the undereducated poor and workers displaced by technology or corporate downsizing to equip themselves for gainful employment.[16]

The United States consumes 14 percent of its GNP on health care, making it the nation's largest industry. This figure is roughly double the share of GNP spent by other industrialized countries on health services, even though other systems are universal and comprehensive in coverage; in 1998, despite the prevailing prosperity, more than 44 million family members of working Americans were without any form of health insurance, and the number continues to grow annually.[17] This vast disparity in resources committed for health care is not reflected, however, in such vital statistics as life expectancy and infant mortality.[18] Nor is there evidence that the quality or reliability of health care is lower in these countries than in the United States, except for longer waiting periods for some kinds of elective surgery. Yet, the United States tolerates the world's most wasteful, cumbersome, and chaotic organization of health delivery, including the byzantine maze of paperwork required by each of the competing insurance companies that finance health care and determine eligibility and term of coverage for subscribers. Physicians and patients find these sets of rules more vexing, more complex, more impenetrable, and more costly than the federal tax code, which is the current target of rightist reformers. Many health providers are compelled to devote as much as 60 percent of their revenues for "overhead" (clerical, accounting, and managerial services)!

Rationalizing the organization of health delivery could save American consumers billions annually that could be applied to other needs. The obvious solution is a single-payer system with standardized eligibility and coverage provisions administered by the federal government or jointly with the fifty states. Individuals, if they wished, could supplement the standard package by private insurance. This idea, first proposed by President Truman in 1948, has been so trashed by intense public relations campaigns by the insurance industry and their allies, who invoke the hobgoblin of government control, that it seems for the moment irrelevant to serious discussions of reform. Progressives, however, should not be intimidated or deterred by these self-serving arguments from advocating the single-payer reform, not when the prospective benefits in efficiency, lower costs, and more inclusive coverage are at stake. The program would be financed by a payroll levy that could be paid by employers, by employees, or shared between them.

The United States already has in place a viable, cost-effective, single-payer, government-operated system, which in 1995 served 37.5 million senior citizens; a very efficient health insurance program for federal employees; and an extensive network of veterans' hospitals. Unit costs of the extended Medicare program could be substantially reduced by emphasizing preventive measures and by the fact that younger people require considerably less medical care than their parents and grandparents. The aforementioned scandal of 44 million working Americans without health coverage and the uncompensated costs to hospitals of emergency treatment for uninsured patients would be eliminated. The present Medicaid program for families below the poverty line could be eliminated if eligibility for universalized Medicare included all persons, regardless of income.

These are national problems, unsuited to market solutions and beyond the unaided fiscal and administrative competence of state governments. The methods to be employed in carrying out these programs, the magnitude of the federal obligation, the contributions of beneficiaries, and the pattern of sharing with states, local governments, private firms, and voluntary associations depend on their relative capabilities and must be negotiated politically. Though these are among the principal targets of the Republican-rightist crusade against the welfare state, they cannot be abandoned by the federal government.

Fifth is the underwriting of opportunities for qualified young people to secure higher education. No talented and ambitious American youngster should be denied the opportunity for postsecondary education for financial reasons. For many families, especially middle-class families whose real incomes have remained flat during the past twenty years, and for talented poor children, the rising costs of higher education have become extremely burdensome, even prohibitive. Federal provision of scholarships, tax credits, and low-cost loans should be available on a sliding scale based on family income to parents and young people who seek technical or vocational education above the secondary level, in effect an extension of the current very effective system of Pell grants. The measures authorized by Congress in 1997 in response to President Clinton's initiatives are modest contributions toward meeting this need. The national interest in a more productive labor force capable of functioning flexibly in a highly competitive, technologically sophisticated global economy is beyond dispute. And so is the principle that opportunities for self-cultivation and self-improvement should be available to all, regardless of family circumstances.

The federal role in strengthening elementary and secondary education has become highly controversial because of the long-standing practice of local control and operation of public schools.[19] The inadequacies of public education, especially the substandard performance of students and graduates, have become the chief concern and anxiety of many American families. The 1994 Contract with America would have dealt with this problem by abolishing the federal Department of Education and issuing vouchers to parents that would divert public funds to finance their children's attendance at private (including religiously sponsored) schools. Aside from its dubious constitutionality, this measure would cripple the American institution of public education by draining off many of the children of more affluent, more influential families and leaving the public schools to deal with low-income and educationally handicapped students.

Clinton's modest proposal in 1997 to fund 100,000 additional teachers, improve teacher training, finance the repair of dilapidated school buildings, and develop national performance standards that would enable local school authorities and parents to evaluate the effectiveness of their schools evoked fierce resistance from congressional Republicans as yet another instance of federal encroachment on local control of public schools. This refusal to address a national need was a clear example of the triumph of ideology over common sense. Progressives must persevere with low-cost measures such as those outlined by President Clinton to enhance the effectiveness of public education without impairing state and local control, since this is clearly a consequential problem that has become national in scope.

Rightist advocacy of educational vouchers has found an unexpectedly favorable audience among African-American and Hispanic parents who believe that vouchers afford them the opportunity to send their children to better and safer schools than those available in inner-city neighborhoods. Various versions of vouchers have been adopted in a number of states and cities, draining resources from the public school system, one of the principal institutions of American democracy.

Innovations and experiments within the system of public education should, however, be encouraged, because they may point the way to improvements in student performance. This applies to certain versions of non-sectarian charter schools that adhere to the same standards of open, nondiscriminatory admission as those mandated for public schools and whose performance is monitored by competent educators.

Education need not and should not terminate with formal schooling; it should be a lifetime quest. It should not be limited to upgrading skills—important as that is in a fast-evolving, high-tech economy— but should be available for individual self-development in pursuit of any branch of knowledge. Providing such opportunities is the responsibility of local public libraries and especially of state and local boards of education whose budgets, however, are stretched to meet the legitimate needs of school-age children. The federal government could help by providing more adequate funding of public radio and television, so that these powerful media could be employed to promote adult education, a function that has been abandoned by the commercial media; and by grants-in-aid to community colleges and local education authorities, labor unions, churches, and other voluntary associations to foster opportunities for adult education.

The sixth in this listing of irreducible federal services is the protection and vindication of rights, mainly of weaker segments of the citizenry, which are guaranteed by the Constitution or by federal statute. These comprise (1) civil rights, especially to political participation and non-discriminatory educational, employment, and housing opportunities for members of racial and ethnic minorities, women, the handicapped, recent immigrants, and homosexuals; (2) the right of workers to organize and bargain collectively, free of the threat of company unions or of replacement workers; (3) the right of consumers to honest advertising and to safe products, and of depositors to the security of the funds they entrust to financial institutions; (4) the right of ordinary Americans to the security of their lives and property, including strict regulation of gun trading and gun ownership, since guns are the principal instrument of violent crime, which impairs the quality of life of millions of Americans. In sponsoring the latter legislation, Democrats would have overwhelming public support.[20] Republicans, by contrast, influenced by the National Rifle Association, which contributes generously to their campaigns, have uncompromisingly opposed any measures designed to regulate interstate traffic in even the most lethal assault weapons.

The seventh item in this list is protecting the environment and conserving natural resources. These closely related services are indispensable to safeguarding the health and quality of life for this and future generations, for husbanding natural resources in ways that sustain their yields, for protecting endangered plant and animal species, and for preserving natural beauty and historic places for the enjoyment of future generations. All such programs have been and remain controversial, because they limit the unrestrained exercise of property rights for economic exploitation. Though the National Park Service, the Bureau of Land Management, and the Environmental Protection Agency have become highly institutionalized and enjoy large, devoted constituencies, they are under continuous pressure to relax their requirements in the interest of commercial "development" or private property rights. Although most of these activities involve federal lands or transcend state boundaries, thus requiring federal management, state governments often supplement federal programs, including the reservation and operation of sites for public recreation.

Managing the Economy

The federal government must attempt to ensure economic stability, the conditions for sustained economic expansion, and the fullest employment of labor and capital consistent with stable prices, environmental protection, humane working conditions, and stewardship of natural resources. The standard macroeconomic instruments available are the monetarist method of regulating the money supply by controlling interest rates, which is a responsibility of the semi-independent Federal Reserve Board; and the Keynesian method of regulating demand by adjusting tax rates and public expenditures. Neither of these methods is guaranteed to work in this era of instantaneous global movements of capital. Interest rate changes may be nullified by the actions of other governments or of investors and speculators, while budgetary pressures may inhibit the employment of expansionist fiscal measures. Congress must be sensitive not only to our fiscal accounts, but also to our foreign trade and payments balances, since, with globalization, international trade in goods and services has become a major component of our economy.

The balanced budget amendment sponsored by the Republican right would block the operation of automatic stabilizers during economic recessions when reduced tax revenues prevent increased spending on unemployment compensation, job creation, and direct assistance to the victims of recession, without resorting to deficit financing. It would shift the entire burden of combating recession to monetary policy administered by the Federal Reserve. Such measures in the past have mitigated the severity of economic downturns.

Except during economic recession or war, the Congress and the president have the responsibility to maintain fiscal discipline, to strive for rough equilibrium between expenditures and revenues and to avoid measures that burden future revenues at a faster rate than expected economic growth, preempting thereby the freedom of future generations to make their own allocative decisions. This may entail the unpleasant responsibility to raise taxes. The failure of Presidents Reagan and Bush, abetted by Congress, to match with additional revenues increased military and entitlement expenditures during peacetime was responsible for quadrupling the national debt, in the period 1980–92, from 33.4 percent of GDP to 65 percent. The legacy of the annual servicing burden approximates $250 billion and would be much higher were it not for the moderate (1998) prevailing interest rates. When Congress and the president are sensitive to the economic implications of the federal budget, this concern counteracts both inflationary and deflationary pressures in the economy, contributing thereby to currency and price stability, investor confidence, and the goals of economic expansion with full employment. The implications of our external trade and payments accounts for federal policy are discussed in chapter 5.

Whatever methods are used, the maintenance of price stability and the promotion of economic expansion are fundamental federal responsibilities, so conceded even by avid free marketers and proponents of minimal government.

Safeguarding the Institutions of American Democracy

The final area of federal responsibilities is safeguarding the institutions of the American political system. These institutions include the rule of law, free and fair elections, open political debate, and the right to petition officeholders. An important contribution to the prevailing public distrust of government has been the unremitting barrage of anti-government propaganda and bureaucrat bashing, the stock in trade of the Republican right during the past three decades.

The recent campaign financing scandals have been, by far, the most insidious threat to public confidence. These scandals have produced widespread cynicism and disgust with politics and government. They have impeached the integrity of the electoral process, a key institution of American democracy. The prevailing public impression is that candidates are forced to obligate themselves to large contributors who, quite reasonably, expect some quid pro quo from successful candidates in return for their generosity. Political operatives in both parties at the national level have been guilty of outrageous, sordid, and patently corrupt practices by the unremitting need to raise large sums to finance political campaigns, notably for the presidency, but also for major governorships and seats in both houses of Congress.

Because Republicans, with their preferential access to wealthy contributors, are conspicuously more successful than Democrats in raising funds under the current loose rules and loopholes, they have resisted any changes in the currently corrupt arrangements, including serious curbs on fund-raising and expenditures by candidates, parties, and interest groups.[21] Among the more egregious abuses are the "soft money" contributions mainly by political action committees (PACs), made ostensibly to express their views on issues, not to support particular candidates.[22] Soft money, however, is obviously manipulated in ways that amount to substantial supplements to competing parties and candidates, yet they are entirely unregulated. In exercising its responsibility to protect our institutions of government and to guard them from the pernicious effects of money politics, the federal government must impose and enforce strict limitations on campaign fundraising and expenditures, including personal funds of candidates and those that cynically circumvent the law by supporting individual candidates in the guise of educating the public by promoting specific issues.

To restore public confidence in the electoral process, progressives must persist with measures to regulate and limit campaign contributions and expenditures from all sources by candidates, party organizations, and interest groups; and to reduce candidates' dependence on private funding by expanding their access to impartially allocated government funds. As a public service in exchange for lucrative licenses for access to the public radio and TV spectrum, station owners should be required to offer substantial free time to candidates for office at all levels of government.[23]

In this chapter, I have enumerated and outlined very briefly the functions that must be undertaken by the federal government in order to respond to the requirements of a dynamic American society and to maintain the American Dream at the outset of a new century and a new millenium. The mere listing of these functions belies the ideology and the campaign of the rightist coalition about the feasibility of shrinking government to the proportions of the mid-1920s. A feasible strategy for conservatives might be to restrain needless growth in government functions by tilting in the direction of non-governmental solutions to the nation's problems or of shared responsibilities among corporations, voluntary associations, and government, where these are plausible options.[24] That approach is a far cry from the fierce attacks on government that have been the stock-in-trade of rightist rhetoric and policy during the past quarter century.

CHAPTER FIVE

Some Continuing Challenges
to Government

Taxes are what we pay for civilized society.
—Justice Oliver Wendell Holmes, *Compania General v. Collector*

Only poor people pay taxes.
—Attributed to Leona Helmsley when indicted
for federal income tax evasion

In the Wake of Prosperity, Unfinished Business

The toll already wreaked by the transfer of manufacturing jobs to low-wage countries, by corporate "downsizing," the weakening of labor unions, and the extension of competitive marketization to more and more areas of American life are well known. Less well known, perhaps, is the crisis in rural America where low prices and overproduction have forced thousands of family farmers, especially in the Midwest, into bankruptcy and liquidation. Since the 1960s the number of family farmers has declined by 75 percent. Republican farm policy, which eliminated set-aside payments that limit supply in order to maintain farm prices, has resulted in the concentration of farm ownership in a handful of megacorporations. These corporations now receive the lion's share of federal subsidy payments that comprise about half of total farm income, further stimulating overproduction, lowering commodity prices, and driving smaller producers to the wall.

Corporations that once demonstrated paternalistic loyalty to the communities from which they sprang and generously supported their civic and charitable institutions increasingly turn their backs on these responsibilities in the interest of their bottom line.[1] The concerns of their shareholders and of the financial markets overshadow concerns for their employees and their communities. The current (1999) celebration of prosperity has restored consumer confidence; reduced price inflation; recorded unemployment and welfare rolls at their lowest levels in two decades; created a boom in entering salaries for college graduates; and eliminated the federal fiscal deficit. But the prospects for many millions of Americans remain precarious, as is demonstrated by the following indicators.

1. *The income gap between the very rich and the middle and lower classes* has become more pronounced than at any time since the 1920s and far exceeds income differentials in any other industrialized country.[2] During the quarter century from 1970–95, the percentage of aggregate real income (adjusted for price changes) of members of the upper 5 percent of taxpayers grew from 15 to 20 percent, while that of the middle 20 percent declined from 17.6 to 15.8, and of the lowest quintile, by a shocking 20 percent.[3] This means that *three of every five American families have not participated in the boom of the 1990s.* Statistical discrepancies of this magnitude disclose opulence at the top, struggle at the middle, and privation at the bottom. They bespeak the breakdown of a sense of national community and solidarity that is highlighted by the coexistence of homelessness, sweatshops, and despair with extravagance symbolized by the walled and gated settlements of the wealthy, complete with their own schools, churches, shopping centers, and country clubs. When such settlements incorporate as separate local governments, their residents avoid contributing taxes to support public institutions and services for middle-class and low-income communities.

Significantly, rightist policy has been oriented to further reduce the tax burden on the wealthy, one factor that, along with a runaway stock market, generous executive compensation, exports of manufacturing jobs to low-wage countries, and reductions in public services for the poor, has accounted for the growing income gaps. No healthy democratic society can long tolerate income disparities of these magnitudes. When Democrats call attention to this fact, they are charged with fomenting class warfare.[4]

2. While the causes of *violent crime*, which preoccupies so many Americans, are many and complex, its high incidence in the United States (despite the welcome reduction in homicides and other violent crimes since 1995) magnifies the sense of insecurity and lowers the quality of life for Americans of all classes. In 1998, 1 American in 150 was behind bars—a rate 5–10 times that of Western Europe and five times the rate in Canada. The prison population has quadrupled since 1980. More than 400,000 are in jail for drug offenses, yet there is no ev-

idence that this mass incarceration policy has curtailed drug consumption. Even the public schools are unsafe, as disturbed children with access to automatic weapons attack fellow students and teachers on school premises. The 1998 rate of incarceration, unmatched in any democratic country, at 668 inmates per 100,000 population, is six times the rate in Canada and has quadrupled since 1980.[5] Spending on prisons to accommodate this flood of convicts has become the fastest-growing element in state budgets.

Violent crime and social delinquency, including the pervasiveness and tenacity of the drug culture, have many causes, including the glamorization of violence in the commercial mass media and popular culture. The sense of hopelessness, resignation, and anger that confronts so many young people from the underclass of American society, the conviction that they have no prospects for decent jobs or family life, for participating in the American dream, is a potent contributor. This is especially true of minority youth in the central cities. The incarceration rate for black males is eight times that for white men. The militia movement and related diffuse expressions of collective hatred of foreigners, minorities, and "the establishment" draw their recruits for political violence from working- and middle-class white families that have lost confidence in the future and are looking for scapegoats.

3. Middle- and working-class youth are no longer confident they can attain the economic status and security that their parents enjoyed. Such pessimism is a threat to the American faith that each succeeding generation would outdo the performance of their parents. Middle-class incomes today are sustained by overtime work—since real wages have barely recovered to 1977 levels—and the dramatic increase, from 33 million in 1979 to 69 million in 1995, in two-wage earner families.[6] Many have become convinced that the Social Security trust fund for which they are taxed will be bankrupt before they retire—an indicator of lack of confidence in the future and in the institutions of American government.

Middle-class consumption levels are increasingly sustained by consumer credit-card debt, which ballooned in 1997 to $3.65 trillion (50 percent of GDP) and continues to escalate.[7] Banks no longer urge depositers to save but rather to incur debt; consumer debt is highly profitable to lenders. The 1997 American savings rate at 2.1 percent was, consequently, lower than at any time in history and shows no sign of recovering.[8] In 1997, a record 1.35 million individuals filed for personal bankruptcy. An economic recession would witness not only a renewal of fiscal deficits at federal and state levels but also a rapid expansion of personal bankruptcies, home mortgage foreclosures, and non-performing bank loans. Similar expressions of middle-class distress would shortly renew demands for federal government action from many sources, including hard-pressed financial institutions, that even market zealots and budget hawks would find impossible to resist.

4. It would be a mistake to conclude that the defeat of Clinton's cumbersome and mismanaged initiative on health insurance in 1993–94 demonstrated that Americans feel secure about their health coverage. Most working Americans are insured by group policies negotiated and financed in some measure by employers. The cost of individual health policies far exceeds the capabilities of working families not included in group policies. As health costs continue to rise at a higher rate than inflation or economic growth, and employers increasingly focus on the bottom line, the medical conditions and procedures covered by insurance are cut back, copayments increase, and some employers have terminated employee health contracts entirely.

For most families, the prospects of serious illness in face of the high costs of physician and hospital care is, next only to unemployment, the principal source of insecurity. This insecurity in turn is exacerbated by the highly publicized attempts of some HMOs to restrict the services they provide in order to maintain profit margins. Disinclined to limit the discretion of business firms and confident that market processes will correct economic abuses, Republican congressional leadership shows little interest in this problem. This presents Democrats with the opportunity to champion the rights of currently insured policyholders and to propose affordable insurance coverage underwritten by the federal government for the millions of working families who have no health protection whatever.

5. *The decline in manufacturing employment* as a proportion of the labor force has aggravated the sense of insecurity and limited opportunity, especially among unskilled and semi-skilled workers. Most politicians and mainline economists prefer not to discuss the *chronic trade and payments deficit,* which exceeded $200 billion in 1998. This deficit persists through prosperity and recession, indicating that for the United States this is not a self-correcting problem. Nor is the deficit likely to be eliminated by the resumption of economic growth in Japan and Southeast Asia. For more than two decades, the United States has

been consuming more than it produces, importing a third more than it exports, relying on foreign savers and investors, mainly Japanese, to finance the annual shortfall by purchasing U.S. government bonds. Repeated efforts by the Bush and Clinton administrations to induce East Asian governments, all of which run large trade surpluses with the United States, to moderate their mercantilist economic policies by admitting U.S. products on a non-discriminatory basis, have been mostly unavailing. The economic difficulties confronting these economies in the late 1990s guarantee that their imports from the United States will decline in value while they attempt, with the help of their devalued currencies, to emerge from recession by increasing exports to the United States. This promises to swell the trade deficit to unprecedented levels.

Economists argue about the causes of this structural disequilibrium and its remedies, ascribing it to macroeconomic factors, such as low domestic savings rates and lagging growth in labor productivity.[9] But surely an important contributor to slow-growing labor productivity and the chronic trade deficit has been the decline in manufacturing employment, caused by the transfer of facilities to low-wage countries and the lack of interest by American entrepreneurs in establishing home-based plants in such key industries as consumer electronics to compete in the large American market. The openness of American markets to foreign products, including those produced by U.S.-owned firms in low-wage countries, has been a major disincentive to U.S. firms to invest in improving the efficiency and productivity of home-based plants. It has been economically rational for them to abandon U.S. facilities entirely. The loss of manufacturing jobs, in turn, has contributed to the decline in real wages for displaced workers; their replacement jobs in the services sector usually pay less than the manufacturing jobs they have lost. This cycle leads to declining opportunity for young unskilled and semi-skilled workers, including those from minority communities, to earn decent incomes. Thus, both at the macroeconomic level—chronic and cumulative trade deficits—and at the level of individual workers, their families, and communities, the decline in manufacturing employment has imposed severe burdens on American society that have not been mitigated by unaided market forces.

The introduction of the European common currency, the Euro, in 1999 heightens the urgency to control and eventually eliminate the U.S. current account deficit. Because the Euro will be regarded as equally safe as the U.S. dollar, when European interest rates equal or exceed those offered by the U.S. treasury, foreign investors will choose to place some of their funds in Europe, rather than in the United States. This trend will force the Federal Reserve to raise interest rates in order to compete for foreign funds to finance our trade deficits, thus slowing the rate of domestic economic activity. The culprit is the chronic trade deficit: benign neglect and self-correcting market forces have failed to reduce it; thus, its elimination must become an explicit policy objective.

Although the ideology of free trade has been institutionalized to the point that any measures savoring of protectionism are taboo, unlimited free trade is not one of the Ten Commandments. Like other policies, it must be evaluated by its fruits. If it begins to inflict too much pain on too many Americans, it will have to be modified or superseded by other policies, not excluding some measures of protection. Meanwhile, there are many positive steps short of protectionism—start-up financing on concessional terms, worker training, product and process research—that federal, state, and local governments can adopt to stimulate and facilitate new domestic investment in industries that employ innovative technologies to turn out entirely new items, or customized products that must be produced near their ultimate consumers, or product lines that would compete in sectors that have been abandoned by U.S. firms. Their domestic sales would reduce the trade deficit while expanding the supply of manufacturing jobs that pay decent wages for high-school graduates.

Neo-classical orthodoxy and its rightist acolytes would condemn such measures as the heresy of "industrial policy," the ominous first step toward government planning and socialism. The sad truth is that neither the Republican right nor the ideological free-trade Democrats have contrived any strategy for coping with the burgeoning trade deficits, which are financed by foreigners who can threaten to unload their massive holdings of U.S. debt and transfer their funds to Euro bonds, reducing the exchange value of the U.S. dollar, and compelling the Federal Reserve to raise interest rates, with negative consequences for domestic economic growth and employment.

It is essential but not sufficient for Democrats and progressives to prescribe and endorse remedies for the legitimate anxieties of the middle classes, such as protecting Social Security, securing medical and health coverage, and providing tax relief and affordable loans for college tuitions. *The poor must not be overlooked or forgotten.* Despite being a demographic minority with low voting turnouts, their numbers are significant. Though the poverty rate has been declining with the prosperity of the late 1990s, at 12.7 percent in 1998 it remained higher than at any time during the 1970s. More than 32 million Americans subsist below the poverty line.[10] One American child in five grows up in poverty and deprivation, with all that this implies in undereducation, wasted talent, and future burdens on public services and the criminal justice system. The number of very-low-income working families who must spend more than half their sub-poverty level incomes for housing continues to increase.[11]

While rightists punish the poor and the weak by slashing the limited government services available to them in order to finance tax cuts, progressives have different priorities. They continue to feel compassion for the disadvantaged and to regard their plight as a test of the moral health of this wealthy American society. To them, the persistence of a large underclass is unacceptable and calls for positive initiatives from government at all levels.

For the working poor who remain in poverty because of limited skills and employment in low-productivity occupations, including low-wage service jobs (hotels, hospitals, food service, retail sales), or in declining industries, measures that would expand the manufacturing sector, raise the minimum wage, provide assured health care, finance reliable and affordable day care, strengthen labor unions, rigorously enforce immigration laws, expand opportunities for job training, and subsidize decent low-income housing can begin to improve their security, quality of life, and future prospects. Such efforts to lift low-income working families above the poverty line require government initiative.

For the dependent poor, many of whom are reduced to social delinquency, drug dependency, and crime, the problems of public policy are far more difficult and complex. The physically and mentally handicapped cannot be abandoned to private charity; their humane care, maintenance, and rehabilitation must remain government responsibilities, though the actual provision of services may be handled by private voluntary agencies. Even though no one is satisfied with welfare as an intergenerational way of life, nobody confidently knows the "answers." Economic expansion plus recent changes in welfare legislation reduced the welfare rolls by 44 percent, from 14.3 to 8 million between

1994 and 1999.[12] The rate of decline has begun to level off; most of the remaining welfare cases are physically or mentally handicapped and thus hard to absorb in regular employment. But the Republican-right approach of dropping recipients from the rolls after fixed time periods could worsen the lot of those who are unemployable and condemn their children to greater privation. Efforts already initiated by the federal welfare reforms of 1996 to reward work and personal responsibility over welfare dependency can restore the dignity and self-esteem of former welfare clients.[13] But first government must invest in their job readiness, in training to acquire marketable skills and work habits, and in health services and day care for working mothers. If private sector jobs are not available, public service jobs must be created, at substantial cost. In the short run, it is less expensive to keep welfare clients on the dole than to invest in preparing them for self-reliance. *The reduction of hard-core poverty cannot be accomplished on the cheap.* The plight of the dependent poor is not amenable to simple and inexpensive fixes, nor can it be mitigated by shifting the burden to state governments.

While it is too soon to evaluate the impact of the 1996 welfare reforms, the onset of recession would force large numbers of ex-welfare clients into renewed unemployment and dependency. What is to happen to those who have exhausted their lifetime eligibility for welfare and to their children when no jobs are available? What will be the social costs of this abandonment of a safety net for this very vulnerable population? The welfare reforms of the late 1990s, with their emphasis on work and on combatting the culture of dependency, have had mixed results and must be carefully monitored. Some former welfare recipients now in the labor market appear to be subsising on subpoverty wages, and some have been eliminated from the Medicaid rolls by state officials, thus denied medical coverage.[14] Measures will be required to correct such unintended consequences of this legislation.

For Democrats to concentrate on the legitimate needs of the middle class is sound strategy politically. But neglecting the poor and the disadvantaged or turning the middle class against the poor and against racial minorities in the expectation of electoral advantage would be morally indefensible and betray their political heritage. (It might also, as we shall see in chapter 8, be politically short-sighted.) Here, too, they must take a principled position that differentiates them from the social Darwinism of the Republican-right.

Federalism for the Twenty-First Century

The American state is organized as a federal structure. Functions that are necessary to maintain the United States as an integrated security, political, economic, and cultural community are assigned to the federal government; residual activities, including those that are distinctively regional and local, are reserved for the states and their local subdivisions. The boundaries between federal and state powers are deliberately flexible and ambiguous, permitting adjustments to changing circumstances and needs. During periods of crisis—wars, economic depressions, and natural disasters—federal powers expand to cope with national emergencies. As the economy has become increasingly integrated and the society has become bound by a common culture, as economic, environmental, informational, and social relationships have become national and even transnational in scope, new functions have been assumed by the federal government, usually in default of the ability of states and localities to deal with them effectively. Thus, during the twentieth century, as the United States has evolved into a more perfect union and assumed a larger role in international affairs, the scale of federal activities has expanded greatly.

It is a mistake, however, to assume a zero-sum relationship between federal and state authority. To the contrary, as federal activities have expanded, so have those of state and local governments. Throughout the twentieth century the states have maintained unchallenged control over a vast array of responsibilities that affect the daily lives of their residents. These include the bulk of civil, criminal and domestic relations law; most phases of law enforcement; elementary and secondary education; most roads, water supply systems, and other public works; regulation of and assistance to all units of local government, including cities; social services; and state police powers, which include the protection of public health, safety, welfare, and morals. The size and scope of state governments have expanded in tandem with those of the federal government. Many functions are shared, financially and administratively, in dense networks involving Washington, the states, local authorities, and often private enterprise in what has been termed by many scholars "twentieth-century cooperative federalism."[15] There is no danger that state governments are about to wither away or that they are being hobbled by federal action.

Economic integration, population growth, technological complexity, and urbanization have imposed greater demands on state governments as well. Since the end of the conservative Eisenhower administration in 1960, federal civilian employment has grown by 20 percent. State and local government employment during these same years has expanded by 160 percent. Federal expenditures have increased by 317 percent, mainly for Medicare, Social Security, defense, and debt servicing, while state and local expenditures together have grown by 341 percent. State and local governments are more active and vigorous than at any time in their history; contrary to rightist jeremiads, their powers have not been usurped, nor have they withered away, nor have they been reduced to mere administrative agents of Washington.

Much cant is abroad in today's public discourse about the remoteness of Congress and federal administrators ("inside the Beltway") from the diverse needs and concerns of the American public and the much greater understanding, sympathy, competence, and accountability of state governments. Little evidence is ever submitted to confirm this populist maxim, and it deserves to be treated with skepticism as a theme of rightist propaganda. The notion that California's state government enjoys an intimate relationship with its 36 million citizens or Texas with its 20 million, different in kind from their citizens' relationships with, say, the U.S. Postal Service, Social Security system, FBI, veterans hospitals, or park service, is far from self-evident.[16] More than 90 percent of federal employees live and work outside the Washington area in the fifty states.

Like its counterpart, the separation of powers within the federal government, the division of powers in our federal system greatly complicates the processes of government, defying all technocratic versions of instrumental efficiency. It has the great advantage, however, of reducing policy and administrative overload on federal institutions, diffusing experience in self-government, allowing for regional and local distinctiveness in public affairs, and encouraging self-reliance in collective problem-solving through institutions that are accountable to regional and local publics. While tensions and conflicts between federal and state jurisdictions are inherent in the structure of American government and must be settled by political negotiation or by the courts, much more common has been the emergence of shared authority.

Frequently, this calls for the negotiation of minimum national standards to entitle states to federal financial assistance in matters ranging from highway construction and maintenance to environmental protection, vocational training, agricultural extension, unemployment insurance, and health administration, with actual implementation by state and local authorities.

The needs and interests of the various states, which are often at odds with one another, are articulated and negotiated by vigorous lobbying in the processes of congressional deliberation and administrative implementation and by day-to-day interstate and federal-state exchanges among professional colleagues. Far from being passive or helpless bystanders, state governments are active participants in both the legislative and administrative phases of their relationships with the federal government. The notion that federal politicians and bureaucrats have ridden roughshod over the states, reaching out and grabbing functions that are properly within the purview of states and localities is a myth hallowed by rightist ideology and rhetoric. Most such functions have been assumed by Washington after considerable hesitation and open hearings in which members of the federal House and Senate, all with local roots and subject to local pressures, decide that the federal government is the proper locus for the effective management of that particular program.

Progressives are committed to maintaining a sound and vigorous balance between federal and state powers and between state and local government. The federal government must not encroach on legitimate state authority, nor should it be stripped of its constitutional responsibilities in the name of states' rights, including its powers to "raise and collect taxes to provide for the common defense and promote the general welfare" and to regulate interstate commerce. Any fair reading of American history demonstrates the abuses and the retrograde practices that have been associated with the doctrine of states' rights, from slavery to the century-long denial of civil rights and constitutional protections of African-American citizens, from repressing labor unions and applying subhuman welfare standards, to gerrymandering legislative seats in violation of the one person one vote principle, and tolerating grossly unequal educational facilities for children from affluent and low-income districts. Many of the landmark victories scored by progressives and their allies for expanded civil rights and social welfare have been bitterly resisted in the name of states' rights.

It is no surprise that the present generation of rightist leaders has rediscovered and attempted to rehabilitate the tattered doctrine of states' rights as a weapon in their ideological crusade for minimal government. During the 1980s President Reagan succeeded in decentralizing a number of federal programs by eliminating federal standards for grants-in-aid to the states and expanding the discretion of state agencies through the device of block grants.[17] Several programs were eliminated entirely, leaving the states with the option of abandoning the programs or financing them from their own resources. The consequent reduction in state services is compatible with the rightist commitment to laissez-faire, low and regressive taxes, minimal regulation, and a social Darwinist morality.

The current enthusiasm for states' rights is manifested in pressures for "devolution" of federal programs, from welfare, housing, and health to environment, labor standards, and civil rights, from the federal to state governments on a much larger scale than those attempted by President Reagan. As with the 1996 welfare reform, reduced federal funds are allocated through block grants to the states to administer under much laxer federal standards. Though states may supplement these funds to improve services, the expectation is that few will do so, resulting thereby in a net reduction of government services and regulation in all activities for which Republicans successfully implement their strategy of devolution. Progressives readily agree that some activities undertaken by Washington, for example, vocational education and the promotion of local economic development, might be transferred to state governments because they are local in scope and the states are competent to deal with them. But these transfers should be deliberated on a case by case basis, not as a mindless, wholesale process. The claim that devolution will increase administrative efficiency is unpersuasive, since there is no evidence that fifty sets of state bureaucracies, individually or collectively, are administratively more competent than the agencies of the federal government.

The diffusion of political power from the federal government to the fifty states, without a concomitant diffusion of economic power, results in the direct transfer of power to giant corporations. The 1990s have witnessed a frenzied rush of mergers among financial and industrial firms, leading to an unprecedented concentration of economic power, with diminishing market competition. The scale of these combinations precludes any serious efforts of regulation by state governments. To the extent the federal government yields functions to the states, it sacrifices the only countervailing power that might protect the public against the abuses of economic concentration.

Republicans have dusted off the Tenth Amendment to the Constitution, which reserves to the states and the people those powers not conferred on the federal government. Since the time of Chief Justice John Marshall (1800–1835), the courts have held that in addition to those powers specifically mentioned in Article I, other powers can reasonably be implied (*McCullough v. Maryland*, 4 Wheat 316–1819). In the exercise of these powers, the federal government cannot be constrained by the reserve clause of the Tenth Amendment (*U.S. v. Jones and Laughlin*, 300 U.S. 1, 1937). Congressional Republicans, with help from a Supreme Court dominated by Reagan and Bush appointees, are attempting to reverse this principle, in pursuit of their ideology of minimal government.

Yet, despite their solicitude for the Tenth Amendment, congressional Republicans attempted in 1995 to shift jurisdiction in tort liability cases from state courts, where it has resided since the birth of the Republic, to the federal judiciary. This occurred at the same time that Republicans were demonizing the federal government and glorifying the states, proclaiming their intention to devolve numerous functions. It was promoted in deference to their corporate constituency, which has objected to large awards granted by juries to plaintiffs in product liability suits in state courts, expecting that the Republican Congress would place limits on the amounts that plaintiffs could claim in such cases once jurisdiction had been transferred. When their agenda requires it and the interests of influential supporters dictate, contemporary rightists seem quite willing to enhance federal powers—to practice devolution in reverse! (Congressional Democrats and President Clinton blocked the enactment of this initiative.)

The Republican right believes that in promoting devolution they are responding to popular sentiment.[18] This can be understood both as an element of American political culture and as the fruits of a half century of concentrated anti-federal government propaganda and bureaucrat bashing. It is perhaps for this reason that neither Democratic politicians nor progressive opinion leaders have found it expedient to take a principled position against the drive for devolution, including stripping the federal government of functions it has performed for many decades. Federal-state relations are a dynamic process, reflecting shifting political forces and changing perceptions about the needs of American society. In the absence of national emergencies, wars, or economic depressions, there are strong pressures promoted mainly in business circles to cut taxes, reduce the regulatory activities of the federal government, and transfer functions to the states. The post–Cold War decade of the 1990s has been such an era. The role of progressives during such periods is to remind attentive publics of emergent national needs that cannot be met by unregulated markets or by the uncoordinated efforts of fifty state governments.

The Republican crusade for states' rights and for devolution is driven heavily by ideology, often in defiance of interest group preferences. In response to rightist attempts to preclude federal preemption of state discretion on labor conditions, environmental standards, women's and minority rights, health measures, consumer protection, and trucking rules, industry representativers frequently lobby in favor of federal action, preferring unitary standards to balkanization of the United States market by fifty different authorities. They argue that the latter increases confusion and raises the costs of their operations without any significant benefits. Labor, environmental, minority, consumer, and health groups generally oppose devolution, anticipating that the majority of states would enact less effective regulations.

Federalism in the United States remains very much alive and well, dynamic and flourishing. There have some abuses by Congress in imposing financial obligations (unfunded mandates) on the states when the latter are called upon to implement federal legislation, including health and safety standards for workers, environmental practices, and civil rights laws. The Republican Congress has, however, brought this process to an abrupt halt.[19] The presumption generally applied in the past has been that functions that can be better handled by the states should remain in their hands. Beginning in the 1930s, the courts have ruled that the reserve powers of the states under the Tenth Amendment cannot limit the federal government in the exercise of its constitutional powers, including its power to spend federal tax dollars to "provide for the common defense and general welfare" (Article I, section 8); Congress and the president are the judges of what the general welfare requires. In the exercise of its powers Congress can determine that an activity should be directly administered by the federal government (e.g., Social Security), by the states under federal standards (e.g., unemployment compensation), or by the states with joint funding by the federal government and the states (e.g., Medicaid). The number of possible patterns is infinite, subject to political and administrative feasibility and bargaining.

Under Chief Justice William Rehnquist, the current Supreme Court, the majority of whose members were selected on ideological grounds by recent Republican presidents, is increasingly employing the federal judiciary to circumscribe the implied powers of Congress and to reassert the autonomy of state governments.[20] A major target of rightist think tanks are conservatively oriented young lawyers, several of whom have already been appointed to federal judgeships and are available for promotion to the Supreme Court. The election of a Republican president in 2000 would almost certainly result in capture of the highest court by jurists determined to cut back the role of the federal government and expand the powers of the states. This could have crippling long-term effects on the ability of progressives to enact their legislative program.

With the populist revival of states' rights, progressives should bear in mind and remind the public that, as its preamble proclaims, the Constitution of the United States was ordained and established by "we, the people of the United States," not by the state governments, and that among the objectives of this historic project were to "form a more perfect union" and "to promote the general welfare." Contrary to the antifederalists of the 1780s, who vainly opposed the constitutional project in their time and whose thinking inspires the Republican right two centuries later, the government of the United States is not a confederal union of fifty sovereignties; that issue was decided by the Civil War.[21]

The Question of Taxes

In chapter 4 I outlined the irreducible federal functions required to meet the needs of American society in the early twenty-first century. Here, I lay out principles for the division and sharing of responsibilities between the federal and state governments. This presentation would not be complete, however, without addressing the critical question of revenues to finance federal operations.

For more than a generation, rightist politicians and publicists have focused their resources on a barrage of propaganda pandering to the public distaste for taxation and identifying high taxes with Democrats. The thrust of this message is that the federal government wastes most of the revenues it collects on welfare, foreign aid, a bloated, parasitic bureaucracy, and massive corruption; and that taxes are a heavy burden yielding few benefits to the ordinary taxpayer. With few honorable exceptions, such as Walter Mondale, Democratic politicians have been intimidated by this theme and offered no principled defense of the need for reasonable levels of taxation if the government services desired by the American people are to be sustained and fiscal deficits avoided. All too frequently they have played the Republican game of bashing bureaucrats, "reinventing" government, and offering competing tax cuts. Moderate left pundits and progressive intellectuals have failed to confront this issue, to come forth with convincing explanations of the need for appropriate levels of federal taxation. The effect has been to feed the ideology of minimal government.

To complicate their predicament, Democrats have been as unwilling as Republicans to target for reduction or elimination the numerous federal subsidies and tax expenditures that serve affluent corporate constituencies, such as access to federal lands at far below market values for the timber, mining, cattle, and energy industries, and the use by radio and television industries of the public wavelengths on highly concessional terms. An estimated $75 billion could be saved annually by the elimination of such "corporate welfare," far more than what might be realized by further reducing services to the poor.[22] Yet, Democrats have either actively colluded in maintaining these lucrative privileges or so feared the political consequences of tackling these well-organized and well-heeled interests that they have failed to place the issue on the public agenda. With few exceptions, intellectuals of the moderate left have avoided this theme.

The notion that Americans are overburdened by high taxes is, by international standards, a myth. Taxes from all levels of government, as a percentage of gross domestic product, are 31.6 percent in the United States. Twenty-one percent is the federal share (70 percent of which is consumed by national defense, Social Security, debt servicing, and Medicare).[23] This percentage is similar to Japan but substantially lower than for any European country.[24] The main difference is that these countries provide and their citizens enjoy universal and comprehensive health care, free higher education, and more complete social services, such as day care, than those available from government in the United States. Though Europeans grumble, have reacted against excessively generous entitlements, and would prefer not to pay taxes at these levels, they realize that the services they expect from government must be paid for. In the United States, politicians of both parties have cultivated the comfortable, escapist deception of the "free lunch": reduce tax levels and revenues will consequently swell;[25] or services can be provided, but someone else will pay.

This populist allergy to taxes in the United States is detrimental to responsible democratic government. As long as the highest priority for public policy is to reduce taxes, progressives and their allies will be helpless. Any proposals to expand and improve public services, even during periods of budget surplus, will be hostage to the political imperative of lower taxes. Current government programs will be starved for funds, not only those addressed to the poor but also eventually such services as Medicare, air traffic control, consumer product safety, and environmental protection, which serve the middle class. New initiatives will be unthinkable.

The absence from Medicare of coverage for prescription drugs is a case in point. It imposes severe hardships on millions of senior citizens because of the very high costs of pharmaceuticals, which are as important to their health as access to physicians and hospital care. Some low-income families must choose between needed medications and adequate diets. Proposals to correct this gap in Medicare coverage would entail modest increases in monthly payments to cover most of the costs of this additional service. Rightist opponents attack these proposals as hidden tax increases. Their supporters should candidly agree that these are indeed tax equivalents but that they are more than justified by very great benefits to millions of senior citizens. Progressives should not deny that such measures are taxes nor shrink from these and similar government programs that meet urgent social and economic needs.

The Republican right have a clear and simple strategy. The keystone is their balanced budget amendment, with its provision that future tax increases must require an extraordinary majority of 60 percent in both houses of Congress. Though narrowly defeated in the Senate in 1995 and 1997, Republicans will continue to promote this amendment because they believe it retains strong public support, even after the federal budget has been balanced without this constraint on fiscal policy. A number of Democratic officeholders, out of honest conviction or intimidation, have supported this measure. If enacted, it would either solidify the goal of minimal government or lead to massive evasion of a constitutional requirement. The framers of the Constitution would have opposed the balanced budget amendment, including efforts to require extraordinary congressional majorities to raise taxes. *Federalist* No. 34, in discussing federal government revenues, contains this passage: "There ought to be a CAPACITY to provide for future contingencies as they may happen; and as these are illimitable in their nature, it is impossible safely to limit that capacity."

A companion goal of the Republican right, in the name of simplifying the impenetrable federal tax code, is to eliminate the modest remaining progressivity in the federal income tax by substituting a flat tax that all taxpayers, rich and poor, would pay at the same rate. Its effect would be radically to shift the tax burden from the wealthy to the middle classes. This has been accompanied by a campaign to demonize, discredit, and even abolish the Internal Revenue Service, thus weakening the federal capacity to collect revenues.[26] Some Republicans would go even further by eliminating the income tax altogether, substituting a regressive national consumption (sales) tax that would further relieve the burden on the wealthy and increase taxes on middle-class consumers. A number of highly placed Democrats are tempted to support some of these "reforms" rather than stand up for the principle of taxation according to ability to pay—the progressive income tax, which has been the keystone of federal tax policy since the enactment of the Sixteenth Amendment in 1913.

Acceptance of taxes adequate to finance needed and desired public services is a moral and political responsibility of citizenship in a democratic polity. The failure of progressive publicists and politicians to support this truism opens the way for rightist propaganda to deceive the American public into the belief that unpopular items such as welfare and foreign aid plus waste and fraud constitute large segments of the budget that could be drastically cut back, thereby financing large tax cuts without affecting other activities such as defense, Social Security, air traffic control, and veterans' services.[27]

President Clinton's courage in 1993 in proposing increased income tax rates for the wealthy as a contribution to reducing the fiscal deficit and restoring some progressivity to the federal tax regime was supported by all but a few congressional Democrats and passed the House and the Senate without a single Republican vote. It was vigorously— and falsely—denounced in 1994 by the Republican right as "the largest tax increase in history." During the 1994 campaign, few Democrats attempted to counter these charges or to explain the rationale for this revenue increase and its benefits to the economy. It is impossible to advocate activist government as necessary to the security and prosperity of American society without accepting the need for substantial revenues and thus of taxation to support the required services.

For rightists, cutting taxes is their patent medicine for all seasons. In hard times they become instant Keynesians: taxes must be cut to stimulate demand. In prosperous times, also, taxes must be cut because government does not need the revenues and politicians will find ways to waste any loose change that comes their way.[28] Democratic politicians continue to be intimidated by the tax offensive. They have declined to meet the tax offensive head-on by insisting that urgent national needs that have too long been neglected—such as improved teaching and upgraded facilities for public education, access to health services for the forty-four million uninsured, prescription drugs for senior citizens, affordable day care for the children of working couples, adequate maintenance of the national parks, modernization of water supply, roads, and air traffic control—should take precedence over tax cuts and even debt reduction. (Since the 1970s, investment in the nation's public infrastructure as a share of GDP has declined by half.) Such claims on public revenues are every bit as legitimate as the claims of Social Security and national defense, which both parties are pledged to honor.

While they criticize Republican tax-cutting proposals as excessive, Democratic politicians of this era have yet to gain sufficient confidence in their priorities to assert, even when there are large revenue surpluses, that such claims on public funds contribute more to the nation's health, prosperity, and well-being than cutting taxes. The intellectual dominance of rightist ideology as described in chapter 2 has been weakened, but not yet reversed.

The Public Interest and Special Interests

Chapters 4 and 5 present and, I believe, confirm the case for an activist federal government which rests on two principles:

1. The well-being of the American nation presupposes a public interest that benefits all sectors of society, transcending the particular interests of any region, industry, class, or organized constituency. Examples of such public goods are national defense, foreign relations, law enforcement, environmental protection, prevention and control of epi-

demics, encouragement of scientific and technological research, maintenance of air traffic safety, preserving the integrity of the currency and of the national financial system, collection and publication of reliable demographic, social, economic, and climatological information, operation of national parks, maintenance of price stability, and promotion of economic growth. This category also incorporates needs that extend into the future beyond the calculations of particular constituencies, such as the conservation of natural resources, space exploration, and public education. Each of these components of the public interest requires the active participation of government.

2. Certain services and regulations that directly benefit particular constituencies qualify as components of the public interest because they provide collateral benefits to society as a whole. These include veterans' services, the network of assistance to agriculture, Social Security and medical care for senior citizens, navigation aids for shipping, student loans, home mortgage guarantees, subsidized low-rent housing, school lunch programs, and promotion of American exports. These, too, require an active role for government. They can be distinguished from government activities that provide services or subsidies to particular constituencies (special interests) but, like subsidies to sugar and tobacco growers or tax concessions to horse breeders, have no beneficial consequences for society.

Chapters 4 and 5 have outlined the categories of services and regulations that are identified with the public interest. They (1) are necessary to the United States as a complex society and integrated economy serving a major world power at the outset of the twenty-first century; (2) must be performed by a legally and politically accountable public authority; but (3) are beyond the unaided competence of fifty state governments. Some of these functions can and indeed are currently shared by networks comprising federal, state, and local agencies, NGOs, and private, for-profit firms.

Because the range of these activities is incompatible with the rightist aspiration for minimal government, states' rights, and continuously reduced taxes, an activist federal government must remain a feature of the American landscape for the indefinite future. The emphasis of politics and statesmanship should be not on disabling the federal apparatus but on continuous efforts to achieve better performance, to upgrade the efficiency, effectiveness, accountability, and responsiveness of federal agencies.

CHAPTER SIX

Not Minimal but Better Government

I have little interest in streamlining government or making it more efficient, for I mean to reduce its size.

—Barry Goldwater, *The Conscience of a Conservative*

For forms of government let fools contest;
Whate'er is best administer'd is best.

—Alexander Pope, *An Essay on Man*

Despite rightist propaganda of recent years, the United States suffers not from too much, but from too little government. The neo-liberal/ laissez-faire paradigm that has dominated public discourse since the 1970s would deprive society of the principal resource available to it to promote individual and collective well-being and protect it from avoidable risks and the abuses of concentrated power.

Take the problems that most concern the public—crime, the drug epidemic, environmental pollution, racial discrimination, job security, substandard schools, dependable health care—all of them require active participation by government, federal, state, local. Many of the failures that have beset American society in recent years—the savings and loan disaster, widespread fraud and abuse of subscribers by health maintenance organizations, creeping monopoly in industry and finance, marketing of diseased and tainted foodstuffs, the flood of illegal immigrants—these have resulted from too little, not too much government. Some of our most gratifying successes—winning the Cold War, exploring space, reducing insecurity among senior citizens, cleaning up the environment, combining price stability with sustained growth—required vigorous and active government initiatives. Some of them involved complex patterns of participation by private enterprise and NGOs, responding to government initiatives, and many were facilitated by complementary state and local government action.

And contrary to rightist propaganda, Americans have demonstrated that they want an active federal government. Americans overwhelmingly desire a strong defense establishment, reliable pensions and medical/health services for senior citizens, clean air and unpolluted waters, strict enforcement of immigration laws, interstate highways, safe and secure air travel, world leadership in science and technology, and timely and compassionate disaster relief. All these are federal services; for FY 1999, they constituted 62 percent of the federal budget net of debt service requirements.

Most of the other federal agencies and programs, such as the National Park Service, Veterans' Administration, Weather Service, agricultural research and extension, Small Business Administration, Occupational Health and Safety Administration, Securities and Exchange Commission, have strong and loyal constituencies prepared to stand up for their maintenance. In principle, American culture remains suspicious of big government and responds positively to rhetoric that denounces it. In practice, Americans favor the major programs that comprise and sustain active government. David Stockman, President Reagan's first budget director, was a zealous apostle of minimal government. Yet, when he left that office, a sadder and wiser man, he concluded: "The American electorate wants a moderate social democracy to shield it from capitalism's rougher edges." [1]

When Americans detect problems in their lives that they cannot handle on their own, they turn to government for assistance: to restrain the abuses of health maintenance organizations; finance more affordable day care; curb gun traffic and tobacco advertising; subsidize student loans; combat the AIDS epidemic; promote free trade or protect American jobs; and, even among fervent apostles of minimal government, control pornography on radio, TV, and the Internet.

The real challenge is not to minimize government or further demonize it but to improve government—its integrity, efficiency, effectiveness, and responsiveness to the needs, preferences, and convenience of the many and diverse publics that constitute the American nation. The intellectual opposition to activist government is based on four charges: that government is an imminent threat to our cherished liberties; that it fosters and protects special interests; that it hobbles economic expansion and efficiency; and that it is inherently wasteful and inefficient. There is merit in such charges, based on ample historical evidence from many governments. In the institutional context of the United States and in its political culture, however, these charges are misleading. They cannot be sustained.

Government as Threat to Liberties

The federal government has from time to time posed grave threats to the liberties of some of its citizens, beginning with the alien and sedition laws in the early days of the Republic. These threats include such events of more recent memory as the World War II internment of Japanese Americans and the controversies stirred by the McCarthy red scare, the Vietnam-era *Pentagon Papers*, Watergate, and Irangate. But despite the damage inflicted by these abuses and coverups, they were eventually brought under control and terminated by the openness and relative transparency of the U.S. government, a vigilant judiciary, a jealous Congress, independent news media, active citizen associations, and assertive public opinion. Their recurrence is possible, but one should not underestimate the powerful countervailing forces in the American political environment. Weighed against the possible recurrence of such threats to liberty is the effectiveness of active government in enhancing and vindicating the liberties and expanding the opportunities of large blocs of citizens who have been historically constrained by discrimination: industrial workers, women, African Americans and native Americans, small investors, and senior citizens. In each case, federal initiatives led the way toward liberating reforms, usually in the face of bitter opposition by apostles of minimal government.

It is instructive to note that many of the rightist charges about government infringements on liberty refer to the concerns of specific constituencies: gun traffickers and gun owners protesting the threat of federal gun control to their Second Amendment rights; corporations asserting their liberty to pollute and to exploit non-renewable natural resources; landlords and employers their freedom to discriminate; tobacco companies their freedom to market addictive and lethal products to teenagers. Public opinion has concluded that abridgments of such "liberties" by the federal government serve public interests that override the complaints of these organized special interests.

Government as Protector of Special Interests

Throughout history, governments have conferred special privileges on favored individuals and groups, privileges based on officeholding, access to status, wealth and incomes, exemptions from legal obligations, or special subsidies and protections. In theory, these privileges are in return for extraordinary services to the state, but more often they are based on patronage and loyalty to a particular regime and frequently they become acquired rights inheritable, like titles of nobility, across generations.

Any legislation that confers benefits on a particular group, for example, affirmative action for racial minorities, price suports for designated crops, access to resources at below-market prices, tax exemptions, or tariff protection, can be classified as "rents," government creation of special privileges. Where these privileges can be justified as serving a public interest—fostering employment, facilitating home ownership, ensuring a stable supply of foodstuffs, reducing racial discrimination—they can be considered legitimate exercises of public authority by a democratic polity. When that line is transgressed (which is often a matter of legitimate political controversy) then the charges of fostering special interests holds, as with corporate welfare cited in chapter 4. These privileges benefit small constituencies but denigrate the public interest and are perpetuated by naked political pressure and large campaign contributions—in effect, bribes.

Contemporary rightist critics of activist government identify as special interests groups that have benefited from government assistance during the New Deal and Great Society eras. These groups include organizations representing racial minorities, homosexuals, labor unions, senior citizens, women, and environmentalists. Such critics exempt from this category organized constituencies that lean toward the right, for example, the Christian Coalition, home builders and land developers, ranching and mining interests, the Business Roundtable, and the National Rifle Association, because they are believed to represent broad public interests. Since many societal privileges are extracted by concentrated economic power, government is frequently called upon to mitigate or terminate such privileges, as in the regulation of monopolistic practices, consumer product safety, and unfair labor practices; or by such positive measures as expanding the supply of low-income housing and ensuring the safety of air transportation. In a capitalist economy, among the most effective controls on the accumulation and perpetuation of special privileges are the progressive income and inheritance taxes, measures that the present generation of rightists are attempting to reverse and even eliminate.

Government intervention can and often does create and protect groups that acquire opportunities, exemptions, and privileges not generally available. Some uses of public authority, such as limiting medical practice to persons trained in medicine, clearly serve the public interest; others, such as the sugar subsidy, serve only to impose hidden taxes on the consuming public. The awarding or denying of such privileges is of the essence of democratic politics; it is the struggle over who gets what, when, and how.[2] The task of progressives is to limit such awards to those that clearly benefit the public beyond the interests of the claimants of these privileges. And since unregulated markets may foster privileges or practices that exploit or victimize the general public, such as fraud, monopolies, polluted air, and substandard wages, government intervention has been found to be essential to protect the public interest.

Inhibiting Economic Growth and Efficiency

Government can, of course, inhibit economic expansion by crude methods such as plunder and extortion, contract violation, state-subsidized competition, and costly regulations; or by more subtle methods such as overprotection, inflationary fiscal practices, or overvalued exchange rates. The methods available to governments to thwart economic development and economic efficiency are legion. Economic history demonstrates, however, that active, not minimal government is a prerequisite to sustained economic growth based on private enterprise and market processes.[3] Government provides police services and legal systems that protect life and property and enforce contracts; it builds and maintains the essential physical infrastructure for the secure and efficient movement of goods and people; and it provides educational facilities that produce skilled manpower as well as technological research and data sources. In addition, it regulates monopoly, maintains economic stability, promotes exports, and avoids competition with legitimate private enterprise. As a business civilization, the United States has confirmed and honored these basic relationships between business and government.

The critical question surfaces when governmental responsibilities for national security; public health, safety, and welfare; conservation of natural resources; protection of the physical environment and of cultural endowments; assuring non-discriminatory opportunities for all citizens; or the need to raise revenues appear to conflict with requirements for economic efficiency. At what point do taxes on corporate income restrain investment, or do pure food and drug regulations retard technological innovation, or do pollution standards raise the price of automobiles? These conflicting values must be reconciled by political processes. When this occurs, rightists tend to tilt toward the demands of business, progressives toward social needs. The result of these frequent clashes of values has been a regime, by international standards, of moderate regulation and a modest set of welfare measures. The continued competitive successes of American enterprise demonstrates that the regulatory, promotional, and service activities of the federal government have not impaired but instead have served as an important stimulus to economic expansion and efficiency. Recall that the quarter century after World War II, an era of activist government, witnessed the most sustained period of prosperity and economic expansion in American history.

Politics, Bureaucracy, and the Absence of Incentives

Critics of government consider it a truism that government is condemned to be inefficient if not downright incompetent because decisions are driven by "politics" and by bureaucratic inertia and self-interest rather than by cost effectiveness. And because government tends to be a monopoly supplier of services, from passports to prisons, it lacks any competitive market incentive to efficient performance. There is no dearth of historical and contemporary evidence of corruption and inefficiency in American government, much of it lurid (e.g., $500 toilet seats; superfluous B2 bombers at $1 billion each; roads and bridges to nowhere). Yet, similar dysfunctions are not unknown to private enterprise, from the massive savings and loan frauds of the mid-1980s to Ford's vast waste of resources in marketing the Edsel, and the bilking of investors in the junk bond market. Whether members of the public embroiled by telephone with credit card bureaucracies in banking enterprises encounter less frustration than when they deal with the Medicare staff is difficult to determine. The results of experiments with privatizing prisons, primary schools, and community hospitals are equally uncertain.

Public service as an incentive plus strict enforcement of accountability can produce a high measure of cost effectiveness and public satisfaction (e.g., Social Security, National Park Service, NASA, Center for Disease Control). Measuring efficiency and determining public satisfaction are no easy tasks in many government operations, such as the Air Force or the Weather Service, where there can be no counterpart to the profit-and-loss bottom line. Most government operations pursue a number of values, of which instrumental efficiency is only one and often not the most important. The American jury system is no model of efficiency in the use of resources; it survives because it serves other, more valuable objectives.

In rightist discourse it is an article of faith that government agencies are overstaffed and wasteful of taxpayer dollars. Such charges are routinely leveled by congress members who criticize the agencies for failing to provide more personalized services to their constituents yet refuse to provide for adequate staffing or to appropriate funds for staff training or for procuring up-to-date equipment. Whether some agencies have more personnel than they need to deliver prompt, convenient, and responsive service is an empirical question. It has been demonstrated, however, that some federal agencies are seriously understaffed. There are too few meat inspectors to prevent diseased meat and poultry from being sold to unwary members of the public, too few air traffic controllers to guarantee air safety at the nation's busiest airports, too few immigration officers to control illegal immigration or to prevent long delays in processing applications for citizenship, and too few labor inspectors to monitor the proliferation of illegal sweatshops. In a number of cities, classes are too large and children are penalized because schools are understaffed. Some of these deficiencies could be overcome by improved technologies or processing methods, but in most cases the upgrading of operations to enforce the laws, protect public health and safety, and provide adequate services require additional and fully trained personnel, and consequently additional funding—more than Congress has been willing to provide.[4]

The charge that government is inherently inefficient is simplistic, often false, and in many instances difficult to demonstrate. It has sufficient merit to warrant the privatization of most commercial-type enterprises producing measurable goods and services that are amenable to competitive market discipline. In the United States, however, there have been relatively few such public-sector enterprises. The pursuit of ever greater cost effectiveness and responsiveness to public needs and convenience outside the market sphere is a continuing challenge to public management, one that is treated in more detail below.

In sum, the case against activist government in the American cultural and political context as a threat to liberty, the creator and defender of special interests, an inhibitor of economic expansion, and a profligate waster of resources is without substantive merit—much rhetoric but meager content. It does not hold water.

Balancing Rights and Responsibilities

There is a moral dimension to the progressive vision of the good society. It holds that there can be no morally legitimate rights without commensurate responsibilities. This theme has been overlooked by the Democratic left in recent decades, which has claimed rights for the more vulnerable segments of American society, such as able-bodied welfare recipients, but has ignored their responsibilities. The Republican right, in turn, claims rights for property owners and businesses, including large corporations and gun owners, while downplaying their social responsibilities. To respect the law, pay taxes, participate in public affairs by voting, and make an honest effort to support oneself and one's children economically are the minimum responsibilities that fall to citizens in a democratic polity. Such obligations should be incorporated into public policy. Many may define their responsibilities more broadly to include caring for dependent parents, assisting needy neighbors, participating in religious affairs, doing voluntary civic work, and engaging in charitable and political activities.

Similarly, business enterprises should define their responsibilities beyond concern for the bottom line or rate of return on shareholders' investments. Corporate citizenship entails the treatment of employees as more than commodities to be bought, used, and discarded on the labor market but as fellow humans investing their skills and energies in the enterprise and entitled to be treated with dignity. Corporate responsibility extends to the communities that depend on them for their economic welfare and even survival. It involves concern for the physical environment and for sound husbandry of the nation's renewable resources, for respecting the moral sensibilities of America's families, and for marketing products that conform to established safety standards. These responsibilities of corporate citizenship have been grievously flauted during the past two decades by some of America's largest enterprises, which have abruptly transferred operations to low-wage countries, downsized and in the process devastated the lives of veteran employees and their families, and reduced thriving communities overnight to ghost towns.[5] In conformity with their laissez-faire ideology, rightists consider such behavior out of bounds for public policy.

Government, in turn, is responsible for using its powers to ensure full employment for the nation's physical and human capacities, including its manpower, and for maintaining price stability that fosters savings, investment, and economic expansion. Its further responsibilities in numerous areas such as national defense and public safety, physical infrastructure, education, labor standards, public health, Social Security, and the environment have been detailed in chapter 4 of this book. These responsibilities form the substance of activist government, which is the core of the progressive version of sound public policy.

The individualist tradition in America's political culture privileges rights as the entitlements of citizens in a democratic republic. The single-minded pursuit of rights by all the active elements of society, individuals and businesses alike, to the exclusion of their responsibilities, would soon reduce civil society to a jungle of competitive self-seeking and impose burdens on the economy and on government that would be impossible to sustain. A regime of individual rights cannot be sustained unless they are disciplined by social responsibilities, and where responsibilities cannot be internalized, they must be incorporated into law. Religious freedom, for example, cannot be allowed to extend to human sacrifice or to fomenting violence against non-believers; nor can freedom of enterprise justify pillaging the natural environment or practicing racial discrimination. Public policy must strive for evenhandedness. It cannot afford to emphasize the responsibilities of one segment of society (for example, welfare recipients, as Republicans are prone to do), while overlooking at the same time the social responsibilities of property owners and businesses; or preach the social obligations of corporations, as progressives are sometimes wont to do, without equivalent attention to the responsibilities of labor unions.

Legislative and Political Initiatives

Americans tend to take efficient, competent, and responsive public service for granted—the friendly park ranger, the hard-working letter carrier, the helpful agricultural extension agent, the reliable monthly veterans' pension or Social Security check, the world-class weapons and medical services available to GIs, the skillful FBI investigator; after all, these are what their tax dollars should be buying. Since Americans are by cultural inheritance skeptical about government, they are attentive to instances in their experience or featured in the media of incompetence, discourtesy, abuse, waste, or corruption; these experiences tend to shape Americans' often-cynical image of "government." Fair enough. Government should be held fully accountable for its performance, to high standards of probity, competence, courtesy, and cost effectiveness—to standards higher than those of private enterprise, which does not use tax dollars. The achievement of better performance by the federal government is, however, a never-ending process for which there are no quick fixes. Some procedures, for example, competitive purchasing or merit-based personnel pactices, are system-wide in the federal government. But most problems that need improvement are specific to individual programs and must be worked out program by program, usually with the cooperation and support of the relevant Congressional committees and organizations representing "stakeholders," the publics who are regulated or served by the particular program. Reforms that are appropriate for Medicare may not be useful for the immigration service or for NASA or the State Department or the Navy. There are many self-appointed gurus and charlatans peddling their special versions of quick fixes to transform the federal government. All should be regarded with suspicion.

I am persuaded, along with most Americans, that the basic institutional structure of the U.S. government is sound. The deliberate diffusion of power through the three branches of the federal government and the division of powers between Washington and the states does retard many decisions and enables determined, often privileged minorities to block majority preferences and often impose their will for extended periods of time, just as southern senators used the filibuster to block civil rights legislation for many years.[6] The cumbersome operations of the checks and balances system often frustrates and tries the patience of some who crave decisive action on matters about which they feel deeply. But the many hurdles that must be overcome before an idea can be transformed into law or policy, the multiple sources of scrutiny, and the many avenues for intervention by the concerned public not only prevent the excessive concentration of government power and protect the rights of citizens from violation by government, but they also avoid precipitous and ill-advised initiatives. Measures that survive this gauntlet of multiple scrutiny and multiple points of access to decision makers are likely to command widespread public support or at least acquiescence. Yet, in times of crisis or national emergencies, the system has demonstrated sufficient resilience to permit prompt and decisive action.

There have been repeated proposals to overcome the diffusion of power in the federal government by converting the institutions of American government to a version of the British Cabinet–Parliamentary system. This was proposed by Woodrow Wilson in 1885, by Harold Laski in his celebrated debate with Don Price in 1944, and by a committee of the American Political Science Association in 1950.[7] Their common purposes were (1) to allow for more effective presidential leadership, (2) more cohesive, responsible political parties that would offer voters clear choices of public policies, and (3) greater accountability that would ensure faithful implementation once voters had indicated their electoral choices. None of these proposals ever evoked significant public support or gained a serious following in Congress.

In every set of complex institutions, problems arise that need to be addressed. Perhaps the most pressing need at the turning of the millennium is to restore public confidence in the nation's electoral machinery, one of the core institutions of democratic government. That this confidence has been rudely shaken in recent years is reflected in diminishing voter turnouts; in the 1996 presidential election, for example, fewer than 50 percent[8] of eligible voters bothered to go to the polls, down from 62.8 percent in 1960. The large sums of money required to conduct political campaigns, much of it for radio and television time and for short manipulative messages and "attack ads," so contrived as to insult the intelligence of serious voters, has compelled officeholders and aspirants to high office to conduct permanent fundraising campaigns, to solicit and accept funds from sources with the most dubious motives, and to be exposed to charges that political favors are regularly exchanged for campaign contributions. The scandals surrounding the 1996 presidential race, especially by the Democratic

National Committee, merely highlight the dependence of candidates on money and the extremes that their managers and supporters are prepared to risk in order to attract and bring it in. Nothing contributes as much to public cynicism about politicians and government as the odor of "money politics," the sense that officeholders are the captives of wealthy financial contributors or self-seeking interest groups. That the current federal code regulating campaign finance is so porous and so full of loopholes as to be entirely ineffectual merely reenforces the prevailing cynicism.

As discussed in chapter 4, the congressional Republican leadership continues to stonewall campaign finance reform, recognizing that their privileged access to corporations and wealthy individuals yields them substantial advantages over their opponents. Yet, the unremitting pressures for fund-raising contaminate both parties and compel all candidates for high office to demean themselves and the offices they seek by continuously soliciting funds. The unfortunate 1976 Supreme Court decision in *Buckley v. Valeo*,[9] that unlimited financial contributions are an expression of free speech, tends to legitimate the current arrangements and complicates prospects for reform. Urgently needed are stringent limitations on financial contributions from all sources. This includes contributions by wealthy candidates to their own campaigns and such transparent evasions as classifying obvious support for particular candidates as issue advocacy, immune from current regulation. To facilitate these limitations on fund-raising and campaign expenditures, radio and TV outlets should be required to allot impartially and free of charge substantial blocs of time to political candidates in both primary and general elections. Until public indignation supplants the current cynicism, however, there is little prospect that this threat to the integrity of our electoral institutions can be redressed.

A number of observers, mainly of progressive persuasion, have deplored the relative demise of grassroots political initiatives and activity. The emergence of top-down, manipulative politics resulting from centralized fund-raising, professionally contrived messages in the mass media guided by sample surveys, public discussions by preselected focus groups, mass mailings based on computerized lists—all these have reduced citizens to the status of consumers of prepackaged advertising bits. Candidates for the highest offices are marketed by the same methods used by the advertising industry to promote underarm deodorants and soft drinks.

Is it possible, in the face of these pressures, to revitalize grassroots politics so that political issues and political candidates can once again originate from the felt needs and concerns of interested citizens as articulated by local labor unions, business and professional groups, environmental clubs, women's associations, senior citizens' and church groups in the many and diverse communities that constitute this nation?[10] The Tocquevillian propensity of Americans to "associate together" in voluntary organizations to achieve common purposes has survived the impact of televised entertainment, with its emphasis on passive and private enjoyment, and the centralization and professionalization of interest-group activity in tandem with the centralization of the economy and of information sources. For the most part, however, despite ritualized encomiums on local initiative from both right and left, and the rediscovery among social scientists of "social capital" embodied in local associations, local bodies now contribute very little to defining the political agenda or to selecting candidates for higher office. Can political parties regain their former role as aggregators of grassroots demands? Would this serve to balance the tendency in our mass society to centralized manipulation to the point that issues are centrally defined by aggressive interest groups, while local associations are given marching orders to throw their weight behind pre-selected candidates at election time? This process likely would benefit the progressive forces aligned with the Democratic Party, but there is little evidence that the energy to spur such activity has begun to emerge from a public disenchanted with and tuned off from politics and political activity.

Public Administration and Program Implementation

While improvement in the performance of government by the legislative route (e.g., campaign finance reform) or by reinvigorating the political process (e.g., grassroots initiatives) remain problematical, much can be done to improve public administration, the operations of the Executive Branch. These operations involve the numerous service and regulatory activities that put government in touch with members of the public and produce most of the complaints about waste, incompetence, red tape, fraud, and abuse on the part of agents of government toward members of the public. Notable examples are Republican attacks on the Internal Revenue Service and Democratic attacks on the Immigration and Naturalization Service. The Clinton administration has attempted to dramatize its interest in this subject by its campaign, led by Vice President Gore, to "reinvent government." [11] This objective has amounted to downsizing by the application of advanced information technologies and contracting some services to private firms; treating the public in customer-friendly ways, following modern business practices; and providing financial incentives (cash bonuses) for superior performance. The Clinton administration claims many successes for its "reinvention" campaign, including the elimination of 300,000 civilian positions in the federal labor force. Academic observers remain more guarded in their assessment of this program. [12] Nor has it succeeded in blunting the Republican-rightist demonization of the federal government.

This focus on reforming and improving public administration in the federal government dates back more than a century. [13] The campaign for a more honest, non-political, more competent, professionalized, merit-based civil service achieved the status of a moral crusade after the assassination of President Garfield by a disappointed office seeker. Its first success was registered in the Civil Service (Pendleton) Act of 1883, which established the framework for a professionalized, merit-based civil service, a movement that was further promoted and extended by the Progressives, notably Civil Service Commissioner and later president Theodore Roosevelt, in the 1890s and early decades of the twentieth century. Shortly therafter, the themes of economy and efficiency dominated proposals for administrative reform, in attempts to introduce into government practices such as scientific management that had succeeded in private business. Given the prestige of private enterprise in America's business civilization, the theme of more business in government has been a prominent feature of efforts at administrative reform, especially under Republican auspices, and has to this day provided lucrative contracts for management consulting firms with established track records in industry, to try their hand with government operations.

The quantum expansion of government operations in the 1930s (the New Deal) and the 1940s (World War II) precipitated a rapid expansion in the career civil service, the development of public administration as an academic discipline, and a set of important innovations in public management promoted by the President's Committee on Administrative Management (1937) and two blue-ribbon commissions under former president Herbert Hoover.[14] These and later studies sponsored by presidents and by congressional committees expanded the understanding of administrative reform to include political and human as well as technical (reorganization, procedures, technologies) dimensions, a pattern that continues to this day. For example, improved operations of the Internal Revenue Service will require more advanced, high-speed information systems (technological), combined with a revised set of incentives for Internal Revenue agents (behavioral), and a more service-oriented relationship to members of the taxpaying public (political).[15]

From this extended learning experience has emerged the current understanding that improved operations in the complex and wide-ranging programs of the federal government must be an incremental and continuous process. The results have indeed been dramatic. One need only compare current technologies used by the average federal agency, in Washington or in the field, with those of one or two generations ago to appreciate that most federal agencies have kept pace with private industry with only minor lags resulting, in many cases, from the reluctance of Congress to appropriate the necessary funds for up-to-date equipment and facilities. Since 1970, despite a 30 percent increase in population, the size of the federal civilian labor force has remained virtually unchanged, at slightly less than 2.9 million.

Progressive politicians and intellectuals must begin to identify not only with more progressive public policies but also with more efficient, effective, and responsive implementation, and with better public administration. Though the Clinton-Gore sponsorship of "reinventing government" incorporated a set of trendy slogans and gimmicks, it nevertheless recognized that it is good politics for Democrats to identify with the need to improve the machinery of government and the delivery of public services. Much of the torrent of criticism and invective against waste, abuse, inefficiency, etc. of federal administration is clearly motivated by Republican-rightist politics and their desire to discredit and disable the federal government. An example is the barrage loosed against the IRS, which seems to be driven less by solicitude for the abused taxpayer than by the determination to eliminate the progressive income tax, to roll back not only the New Deal but also the Progressive movement of the turn of the twentieth century.

Nevertheless, a diffuse enterprise that collects from the public and spends annually $1.7 *trillion,* or 21 percent of GDP, which regulates many aspects of daily life and provides numerous services, needs to be continuously scrutinized for opportunities to increase the efficiency of resource use consistent with the rights and convenience of citizens and the fair treatment of government employees. As stewards of these resources, the government is obligated to ensure and account for their honest, lawful, and efficient use; this is a role that contemporary progressives in and out of government should readily embrace, as they did during the Progessive era earlier this century. While some opportunities for improved operations may be approached by overhauling government-wide systems such as personnel and financial management, most must come, as I have previously noted, from attention to each of the many and diverse activities supported by government. In some instances, this may require action by Congress, to revise enabling legislation (e.g., to permit the use of sampling in the decennial census), to appropriate additional funds (such as for high-speed computers for the air traffic control network), or to revise and simplify procedures (e.g., contracting methods in the Defense Department). Most progress, however, depend on upgrading the standards, the morale, and the incentives of federal personnel, which were badly damaged by the bureaucrat-bashing that was the stock in trade of the Reagan-Bush years and has not been effectively counteracted during the Clinton presidency. "Federal bureaucrat" has become a term of derision in contemporary political discourse, with Republicans believing that it is enough to dismiss any proposed government initiative, from the supervision of health maintenance organizations to the expansion of day care facilities by noting that they would be administered by "some government bureaucrat in Washington."

Where there is government, there must perforce be administration, and administration is operated by men and women. The more carefully these men and women are selected, the better they are trained for their responsibilities, the stronger their morale, the more positive their incentives, and the more effective their performance is likely to be. Given the trashing of government and the civil service during the past two decades, it is not surprising that so few of the brightest and the best look to government for their careers. The disincentive is less salaries than prestige, because many positions in government afford far more interesting and consequential work than comparable positions in private enterprise. Though salaries are generally far lower, especially in professional and managerial ranks, many professionals are motivated more by opportunities to practice their professions in challenging and socially useful work than by money. Otherwise, NASA, the Centers for Disease Control, the foreign service, and the Federal Reserve would be unable to attract and retain their very able personnel, which suggests that efforts to stimulate performance in government by applying such business practices as special financial incentives (bonuses) are beside the point; most people who choose government as a career are motivated primarily by other values.

The not-so-secret key to improved government operations—excluding the legislative authorizations and the congressional appropriations previously noted—is better performance by government personnel. Better performance is facilitated by a higher order of public respect and recognition than has been available in recent years. Promoting such respect is the responsibility of journalists and commentators with progressive sympathies and of senior officials, including the president and his immediate aides, who must recognize that the effectiveness of the programs they sponsor depends in large measure on the morale of the civil service, which is subject to constant carping by rightists who regard the civil service as surrogates for activist government—the target of their policy. Restoring public respect for government will attract more talented recruits. These should be accorded greater opportunities for advanced training and investment in their professional development, along with greater exposure to managerial skills and insights than have been available for any but military officers in the U.S. government.[16] Government personnel need to be provided with technical support, mainly in the form of advanced equipment relevant to their particular programs, since these are prerequisite both to improved productivity and more responsive service.

Finally, the principle and practice of participatory management engages the knowledge, information, energies, and enthusiasm both of rank-and-file staff and of organizations of the publics who are served or regulated by federal programs. Participatory management taps the first-hand knowledge of staff members, who are close to operations and of the public stakeholders who are directly affected; they enable federal agencies to take account of field conditions and accommodate operations to local needs, preferences, and convenience before they become issues of contention. As such adjustments to local publics or to state and local officials may require changes in agency policies or even in legislation, these requirements can be signaled by the operations of participatory management. Some such proposals may, of course, raise contentious clashes of interest that cannot be resolved by administrative processes but only by political action involving Congress and the political levels of the Executive Branch.

Proponents of activist government are interested primarily in substantive policies and programs that draw on the resources of government to increase productivity and enhance security and quality of life for the American people. But the success of these programs may stand or fall on processes of implementation, on the way they are administered. For this reason, a share of the energies and the attention of progressives needs to be committed to the less glamorous but no less essential questions of administrative management. As I have noted, serious attention to this need has been diverted by the attraction of trendy quick fixes, mainly getting government to work like private firms. The latest such nostrum, also promoted by Vice President Gore, is Performance-Based Organization (PBO), a means for setting quantitative output goals for many government agencies and hiring executives competitively to manage these agencies, but subject to dismissal if they fall short of their goals and to generous bonuses if they fulfill or exceed their quantitative targets. PBOs would be relieved of statutory obligations to conform to government-wide personnel, procurement, and accounting standards in order to operate more like private firms in competitive markets. The short history of these initiatives has not been encouraging because they fail to appreciate the fundamental differences between private enterprise and government.[17] What may be eminently rational for a profit-making firm may not be rational at all for a democratically responsible and accountable government agency.

Government agencies, especially in the United States with its regime of checks and balances, are subject to multiple forms of accountability unknown to private enterprise. These controls are deemed necessary to protect probity, transparency, and conformity with law and with government-wide standards of equity; they are enforced not only by departmental control agencies in the executive branch but also by vigilant congressional committees and often by the courts. Moreover, they are subject to continuous scrutiny by politically active and often influential interest groups. Any relaxation of these controls, except in time of national emergency, even in the name of increased efficiency, are received with suspicion by these multiple points of control, which explains why the much-heralded movement toward PBO—and similar initiatives in the name of instrumental rationality—yield such meager results.[18]

Serious efforts to increase the productivity and cost effectiveness of federal agencies must take account of the political environment in which they operate in an open democratic polity. To some pharmaceutical manufacturers, procedures employed by the FDA before authorizing the marketing of new products are harassing, time-consuming, and wasteful; to consumer organizations, these same procedures are applauded for rigorously protecting the health and safety of patients. When the Census Bureau proposes to use sampling methods to correct undercounting in the decennial census, they are credited with using the latest technologies and simultaneously denounced for violating long-standing requirements for counting household members one by one. Does sampling represent good administration or bad administration? Democrats tend to welcome sampling because it raises the count of minorities, who are harder to reach by the traditional methods and who lean toward the Democrats; Republicans oppose sampling for those same reasons. Both claim they are supporting sound public administration.

Yet, over the years numerous improvements have been achieved in the productivity of government operations, usually incrementally, on an agency-by-agency basis. Cumulatively, over time, they have transformed government operations. A few programs and agencies have been allowed to lapse and have been eliminated; some have been privatized. Numerous services, from lunchrooms to libraries and prisons, have been contracted out, with uneven results. It can be confidently predicted that the quick fix of the 1990s—"reinventing government"—like such earlier highly touted enthusiasms as PPBS (planning, programming, and budgeting system) in the 1960s and scientific managment in the 1920s, will pass quietly into history, leaving little of consequence in their wake, while the steady and patient program-by-program, agency-by-agency efforts to improve the cost effectiveness and responsiveness of government operations will persist.

The unremitting rightist campaign to savage government and caricature government personnel (bureaucrats) has little to do with the efficiency of government performance and much to do with their determination to discredit government by undermining public respect and support. As the goals of progressives and their allies require activist federal government, Democratic politicians and publicists need to sponsor and sustain a vigorous defense of government, of the services that government provides, and of the men and women who embody these services, from school teachers to park rangers and the anonymous civil servants who ensure that Social Security checks are delivered with total reliability every month and that the medicines Americans buy for themselves and their children are safe and honestly labeled. An important component of respect and appreciation for government is the assurance of accountability, that its operations are managed with due concern for probity, economy, and responsiveness to the needs and convenience of the public.[19] Following the precedent of their Progressive antecedents, who promoted civil service reform and economy and efficiency a century ago, today's progressives must advocate and identify themselves with effective implementation to ensure the viability of enlightened policies and programs.

The ultimate success of a progressive program of socioeconomic services and regulations will depend as much on government's capacity to implement such activities as on political skills in securing their enactment and protecting them from opponents. For this reason, progressives must concern themselves with building, sustaining, strengthening, and defending the administrative capabilities of the federal government.

CHAPTER SEVEN

The Progressive Coalition:
Elements of a Winning Strategy

> Equality of opportunity for youth and for others
> Jobs for those who can work
> Security for those who need it
> The ending of special privileges for the few
> The preservation of civil liberties for all
> The enjoyment of the fruits of scientific progress in a wider and constantly rising standard of living.
>
> —FDR, "An Economic Bill of Rights"

Policies, however enlightened, remain sterile unless they can be implemented politically. Here I discuss strategies for implementing a progressive agenda that would reinvigorate American democracy and prepare American society for the challenges of the twenty-first century. At the heart of this agenda is the need for active, responsive government.

The Progressive Intellectual Predicament

At the time of this writing, Democrats and progressives are in an intellectual quandary. Despite their clumsy tactics and internal stresses, the Republican right is firmly anchored to free market/anti-government doctrine that has become hegemonic in recent years, enabling them to control the public policy agenda even when they lost the presidency. Clinton regained the presidency for the Democrats by exploiting Republican bumbling on economic matters and coopting such rightist themes as crime fighting, balanced budgets, welfare "reform," and free market economics. While Republicans predictably run against government, Democrats are confused and divided. Some join President Clinton in celebrating free market economics and proclaiming the end of the era of big government; others attempt to revive the spirit of FDR's Economic Bill of Rights, which implies an active role for the federal government.[1]

Progressive intellectuals have done little to relieve this confusion. They, too, have split between those who accept neo-liberal globalism while attempting to adhere to progressive social values, and those who remain committed to government initiatives in the economy and the Keynesian-limited welfare state paradigm that came to fruition in the 1960s. Unlike the right, which patiently developed, refined, and propagated a coherent alternative paradigm, many intellectuals associated with the moderate left have been content to refine their familiar ideas and programs on the margins. Others have been drawn to identity politics and single-issue causes such as feminism, environmentalism, racial equality, and homosexual rights.[2] Moderate-left ideas emphasizing solidarity, compassion, tolerance, and public virtue, which a generation ago inspired young people and dominated discourse in the media and on college campuses, have given way to rightist principles. These are aggressively cultivated by well-financed right-wing campus journals that ridicule "political correctness," promote traditional morality and individualistic self-interest as the appropriate ethos for the current era, glorify market processes, and condemn government for corruption, incompetence, and gratuitous meddling in the affairs of individuals, families, and especially businesses. The response from left-leaning intellectuals has lacked the passion, the assurance, and the coherence of the rightist attack. Until this disparity has been overcome, until progressives find their bearings under the political conditions of the early twenty-first century and regain their intellectual self-confidence, they cannot recover politically.[3]

The heart of the Republican-rightist intellectual initiative and the stumbling of the moderate left concern the appropriate role of government—the subject of this book. Even the evangelical right, which calls on the state to enforce their moral agenda, participates in the denigration of government. This is the issue that progressives must address as their forebears did a century ago. They cannot rely on the excesses of the Republican right, such as their closing of the federal government in 1996 and the impeachment spectacle in 1998–99, to regain the political initiative. Chapter 4 elaborated my conception of what the role of democratic government must be if twenty-first-century America is to be properly served. This chapter outlines a strategy for the intellectual and political fufillment of that design.

A strategy to recover majority support that will, once again, enable progressives to determine the agenda of American political discourse must draw on a set of values, of moral principles to which individual policies and programs are anchored. Nothing has been as bizarre in recent political discourse as the appropriation of "values" by the Republican right as they celebrate unrestrained cupidity, self-interest, and social Darwinism at the expense of ordinary citizens. In response, Democrats and the intellectuals and publicists who support them must cease justifying their initiatives solely in terms of the self-interest of groups of their constituents. Like the Progressives of a century ago, and like FDR's Economic Bill of Rights, Martin Luther King's civil rights movement, and Johnson's Great Society—like all the great reforms in American political history—their initiatives must be rooted in a higher morality. Their vision of a more just, virtuous, equitable, and inclusive society must be explained and justified in those terms. It must inspire Americans, especially American youth, to set aside their current cynicism, self-absorption, and fixation on personal-materialistic goals so that more generous concern for their neighbors, passion for justice, and confidence in their public values can be reflected in public policy and in the environment of public affairs.

A robust commitment to the improving society should be informed by and aspire to realize the values of *inclusiveness*, or equal opportunity and fair treatment for all, that none should be left out of the American dream; of *solidarity*, that all Americans who find themselves in difficult straits for reasons beyond their control have legitimate claims on sympathy and a helping hand from government acting as the agent of the American nation; and *personal responsibility*, that all able-bodied and mentally competent adults are expected to make an honest effort to support themselves and their families economically and contribute according to their means to the common needs of their community and nation. Inclusiveness, solidarity, and personal responsibility are to be realized within an institutional framework that defends and promotes individual liberty and social justice. These values underlie the five operating principles of the progressive vision for America as set forth in chapter 1.

I have not alluded to patriotism as a proud legacy of the progressive movement, but it remains as relevant as it was a century ago. Love of country presupposes a determination to protect its core values and its way of life, a willingness to defend it against foreign threats and even to pay the ultimate price. Patriotism has nothing to do with bombastic chauvinism or contempt for foreigners. Genuine patriotism entails a desire to husband our natural endowments for present and future use and enjoyment, to sustain the quality of the physical environment, and to improve opportunity and the quality of life for all members of the American nation, while safeguarding their human rights.

Patriotism is more than an abstract attachment to a nation's institutions and values. It implies, as well, a concern for fellow citizens of all backgrounds and all classes, a concern that they be treated fairly, that their needs be respectfully acknowledged, that the pain they feel be mitigated as far as possible by whatever agency, including government, is best equipped to lend a helping hand. This concern is felt especially for underdogs, those who are least able to shift for themselves—the handicapped, the elderly, the unemployed, single mothers, and disadvantaged children. While they are grateful for the many blessings of American democracy, progressives are sensitive to situations in which our national performance falls short of our national ideals and our national capacities. Progressives are capable of moral indignation when these shortfalls create needless injustice, insecurity, or suffering—for example, 44 million Americans with no health insurance; overcrowded, underequipped, and unsafe public schools; 35.6 million Americans subsisting below the poverty line—and capable as well of determination to rectify these deficiencies by whatever means are available.

Since World War II, progressives have unwisely allowed rightists to appropriate the mantle of patriotism and bend it to their partisan needs. Democrats have allowed opposition to specific provisions of foreign policy—the Vietnam War, patronage of repressive Third World regimes, the military expansion of the 1980s, including the Star Wars fantasy, and the tendency of some left-leaning intellectuals to take a relaxed view of Soviet intentions—to expose them to rightist charges that impugn their patriotism. If progressives are to win back the allegiance of the American majority, which they enjoyed in mid-century, they must demonstrate that they share with that majority their healthy love of country, its accomplishments and institutions, and must aspire to realize in practice the values enshrined in its great public papers. Patriotism is individual self-esteem writ large.

The Progressive Renewal: Basic Themes

Of vital importance are the themes that must inform the practical realization of these values during the next few decades. Whether these values will be realized depends on the intellectual and political revival of the Democratic-progressive coalition. None of these themes are entirely new. Some are traditional standbys of American progressivism, a few are fresh; together, they constitute a principled paradigm for responding to the country's needs in the years ahead and providing a sound platform for a winning coalition.

Fiscal Responsibility

The first of these themes is fiscal responsibility. The need to balance revenues and disbursements is one of the fundamental principles of responsible governance. While this principle can be abridged to cope with emergencies, such as war and economic depression, such lapses cannot long continue without stimulating inflation, depleting the national savings pool, risking high interest rates, and threatening economic stability and the exchange value of the dollar. There is strong temptation for politicians to tolerate fiscal deficits, as voters enjoy and demand expanded public services but resist the taxes to finance them. The recurrent expenditures of government for operations and services, including defense and the major entitlement programs, should be financed from current revenues; progressives must face up to the need to provide such funding when required.

The traditional discipline of balanced budgets was undermined by the Keynesian theorem that prescribed fiscal stimulus to activate lagging demand in times of economic recession (and, conversely, cutting expenditures or raising taxes and interest rates to curb excessive demand in boom times). But Keynes did not challenge the need for fiscal balance during multiyear cycles. Since the 1930s, Democrats and progressives have been vulnerable to the charge of fiscal profligacy—tax and spend—because the New Deal involved deficit spending to cope with the Great Depression, followed by heavy borrowing to finance World War II. Beginning in the 1950s, many Democrats became convinced that the United States had entered the era of the affluent society, of ever-expanding growth, that fiscal deficits could be tolerated without adverse effects on the economy, and that desirable services and investments that meet public needs or improve quality of life need not be postponed for fiscal reasons. Thus, the American economy absorbed modest deficits painlessly until the Vietnam War, financed largely by borrowing, began to contribute, along with the oil shocks of the 1970s, to double-digit inflation, which was finally counteracted by sharp rises in interest rates engineered not by Congress but by the unelected Federal Reserve Board. High interest rates contracted the economy and precipitated the deep recession of the early 1980s.

The tax-and-spend label has been so identified with Democrats that when President Reagan financed deep tax cuts for upper-income taxpayers and a massive military buildup by fiscal borrowing, creating unprecedentedly large deficits and debt accumulation, he escaped public criticism. At the same time, he attacked the Democrats as free-spending liberals and sponsored, with a straight face, a balanced budget amendment to the Constitution![4] That charade continued through the Bush years, pushing annual deficits and the cumulative public debt to unsustainable levels that depleted the U.S. savings pool and depended on foreign investors for financing.

President Clinton performed a valuable service for the Democratic Party for his role in bringing the federal budget under control—converting a $290 billion annual deficit in FY 1993 into fiscal surpluses beginning in 1999. Democrats can no longer be tagged convincingly with the tax-and-spend label. But if they are to benefit from their new identification with fiscal rigor, they must be prepared to face up to the issue of taxes, as discussed in chapter 5. Republicans can be counted on to plump for ever-lower taxes, to advance their ideological goal of minimal government and because they consider the tax issue their strongest and most reliable electoral weapon. But if Democrats are to support the expanded public services outlined in chapter 4, they must find the necessary revenues. Some revenues may come as dividends from economic expansion, but others may require supplemental taxes. (Recapturing the estimated $75 billion now squandered on corporate subsidies is, of course, a tempting initial target.)

Public investments, long-lasting facilities that enhance economic productivity, include the public infrastructure: highways, seaports and airports, water supply systems, mass transport facilities, as well as school buildings, low-cost housing, and public recreational sites. The financing of such facilities is governed by a different logic. Since they yield benefits over extended time periods, they can appropriately be financed by public borrowing. The scale of such debt financing must, however, be controlled to ensure that the public debt expands at a lower rate than the anticipated growth in GDP. The national debt, while growing in absolute terms, would continue to decline as a share of national output. Thus, the annual burden of servicing the debt would also decline.

The unexpected fiscal surpluses experienced in FY 1999 and projected for the future opened a fresh chasm between Republicans and Democrats. Predictably, the Republican leadership proposed to consume the surplus on across-the-board tax cuts that would benefit primarily the wealthy including elimination of the inheritance tax. President Clinton proposed that the bulk of the surplus bonanza be committed to fortifying the Social Security and Medicare trust funds to ensure their solvency well into the twenty-first century. Unable to oppose these initiatives, Republicans have been forced to scale back their proposed tax cuts.[5] Clinton is right to resist tax cuts, since the first signs of recession would diminish and perhaps eliminate the surpluses altogether.

Democrats must continue to advocate the principle of taxation according to ability to pay. This has been the rationale of the progressive income tax that prominent rightists are now attempting to eliminate. They would substitute a single, flat-rate income tax—taxing the rich and the poor at the same rate—or replace the income tax entirely with consumption taxes. The effect of both would be to shift the tax burden even further from the rich to the middle classes, consistent with rightist tax policy since the 1980s, which has contributed to producing the most skewed distribution of income in our recent history. In addition, prominent members of the Republican congressional leadership have advocated eliminating the earned income tax credit that benefits the working poor and using the savings to lower inheritance and capital gains taxes—a direct transfer of income from the poor to the rich.

Progressives must base their fiscal policies, proposals, and behavior on four sound principles: (1) fiscal responsibility and budgetary discipline, that is, a commitment to balancing recurrent expenditures with current revenues; (2) the need to finance additional government activities with commensurate additional revenues; (3) public investment, to be financed where necessary by borrowing but on a lesser scale than anticipated growth in national output; and (4) taxation according to ability to pay, which means preserving and strengthening the progressive income tax while eliminating subsidies that privilege special interests and make no evident contribution to public welfare. Some adjustments in the tax code are required in the interest of equity, where income increases in moderate-income families propel taxpayers into brackets that increase their tax obligations well beyond their income growth.[6]

It is important to avoid encumbering future years' recurrent budgets with obligations that expand at a higher rate than future revenues, thus preempting the choices of oncoming generations. For that reason, progressives must face up to the need to restrain the future built-in expansion of expenditures for the major entitlements, especially Social Security and Medicare.

Economic Expansion

The progressive coalition must, as Democrats traditionally have, speak the optimistic language of economic expansion and prosperity. But their concept of economic growth differs from the Republican right's embrace of that concept in two important respects: expansion must be compatible with protection of the natural environment and the prudent stewardship of natural resources; and the benefits of growth must be equitably distributed among workers, owners, and consumers within the framework of a full-employment economy. For example, the minimum wage should be converted into a living wage, raised to the point that no family whose breadwinner works a full, forty-hour week should be compelled to live in poverty.

Equitable distribution of the nation's abundance should provide the material foundation for basic security and a minimum of the amenities of modern life to all families and individuals. Many progressives are repelled by the current emphasis on mindless, frantic consumerism promoted by unrelenting, high-pressure commercial advertising in the mass media and fueled by easy consumer credit that has expanded to dangerous levels and addicted many individuals and families to consume beyond their means.[7] In addition to satisfying their material needs, economic growth should enable all who are so inclined to cultivate their spiritual, cultural, intellectual, and professional development. It should enable government to expand public services such as education, environmental protection, parks and recreational facilities, and leisure-time activities that improve quality of life for all members of society. These subthemes are morally and politically powerful, thus sources of vulnerability for rightists, who have shown little interest in any of them. They have been prepared to weaken environmental and resource management regulations in the interest of short-term exploitation of resources. And they presided without any expression of concern over the deterioration in the distribution of income from 1981 to 1993.[8] Rightists oppose modest, periodic increases in the minimum wage, which in real terms fell from the equivalent (in 1996 dollars) of $6.47 per hour in 1970 to $4.75 in 1996.[9]

The economy has expanded at a steady, moderate pace during the Clinton years, steady enough to reduce unemployment to its lowest point in three decades, and moderate enough to control inflation, lower interest rates, and spur investment in home construction and industrial equipment. In two important respects, however, the economy has been deficient: labor productivity has increased very slowly, and these increases have not been distributed equitably to working people. Gradual and sustained advancement in material living standards depends on increasing labor productivity, plus its fair distribution. Increasing labor productivity depends on more efficient industrial and office machinery, on innovative processes, on a continuous stream of new products, and on the skills and motivation of the labor force. In the context of America's high-wage economy, these new products must be based on advanced skills and complex equipment because low-skilled, labor-intensive work has been transferred irreversibly to low-wage economies overseas—often, unfortunately, at high cost to American workers, their families, and their communities.

To stimulate higher productivity and innovative products, the federal government must increase its annual investments in the basic sciences, for these are the keys to facilitating high-tech industries, maintaining America's economic competitiveness, increasing living standards, and restraining the current unsustainable trade deficit. Government should provide strong fiscal incentives for the private sector to invest in developmental research, counteracting Wall Street's pernicious preoccupation with the short-term bottom line that has been imposed on so much of American management in recent years. Despite hand-wringing from rightist ideologues and conservative economists, government should sponsor industrial policies that promote manufacturing, because this sector remains an important source of decent wages and secure employment for high-school graduates, who have yet to benefit from the current prosperity.[10] Indeed, it is unlikely that the pervasive social delinquencies that ravage so many of our low-income communities can be alleviated without the prospect of decent jobs for men and women with limited formal education.

Wage earners are entitled to a fairer distribution of increases in productivity than they have received in recent years. As previously indicated, while productivity has increased by 25 percent during the past quarter century, real wages for semi-skilled workers have declined.[11] The difference has been captured in the form of corporate profits or executive compensation.[12] The weakening of labor unions, beginning with President Reagan's measures that broke the airline controllers' strike in 1981, is a major factor in the stagnation of labor rates, plus high rates of immigration combined with fear on the part of workers that wage demands will result in downsizing and the exporting of their jobs. A labor-friendly administration would offer positive support to labor unions and penalize enterprises that export American jobs with the intention of importing their products tariff free into the United States. It would invest public funds in helping workers upgrade their skills so that they can compete for jobs that require higher levels of skill and pay higher wages. Many such jobs continue to go begging during the late-1990s era of low unemployment.

Government policy cannot afford to be paralyzed by the ideology of free trade, which is vigorously promoted by neo-liberal ideologues and multinational enterprises. Organized business has taken advantage of globalization to reverse the terms of competition with labor for the distribution of the economic product by undermining the welfare state, weakening labor unions, and transferring operations to low-wage countries. U.S. policy elites, including the Clinton administration, appear to be content to allow the logic of economic globalization, as though this were an irresistible natural phenomenon, to determine U.S. government policy without deploying any of the resources available to a government with jurisdiction over the world's largest economy. Continuing pressure to open foreign markets to American products remains essential but insufficient; it has failed to reverse the mercantilist and protectionist policies of Japan and China, which account for the bulk of the burgeoning U.S. trade deficits. The opening of foreign markets must be accompanied by measures that promote investment in the United States in new products and advanced technologies oriented to domestic markets, to win for American firms and American workers home markets for relatively complex and sophisticated products that require customization for sophisticated American consumers or employ technologies that require a well-trained and therefore well-compensated labor force.[13]

Overcoming the current laissez-faire/free trade orthodoxy will require an aggressive campaign by progressively oriented intellectuals and writers to pave the way for Democratic politicians. Fortunately, this has potentially a powerful appeal, as demonstrated by the success of House Democrats in the fall of 1997 in defeating the fast-track proposal for trade legislation, despite aggressive lobbying by multinationals and the White House. This issue should not be abandoned to crude economic nationalists such as Pat Buchanan or populists such as Ross Perot. Controlling the trade deficit is not an expression of economic nationalism; it is, however, essential to America's enlightened self-interest and the health of the American economy. Expansion that focuses on manufacturing industry, using time-tested methods of financial incentives combined with upgrading labor skills, can be both economically rational and politically potent while avoiding the stigma of protectionism.

If the current prosperity should falter, if economic recession should recur and unemployment increase along with underutilized production capacity, the federal government will once again be called upon to stimulate demand by a combination of monetary and fiscal policy involving reduced interest rates and higher public expenditures. That compensatory fiscal policy on a moderate scale is again conceivable can be credited to recent successes in controlling the federal budget deficit. The current euphoria over projected trillion-dollar surpluses and debates on how the bonanza should be spent would quickly evaporate in the event of an economic recession. Federal expenditures under recessionary conditions increase automatically to cope with increased demand for unemployment compensation and emergency assistance. These expenditures should be accompanied by increases in wealth-producing capital projects, in major and minor public works, the former to close the growing gap in the nation's transportation infrastructure, the latter as grants to local authorities to rehabilitate dilapidated schools, water supplies, and sewage facilities and increase the supply of affordable low-income housing. Once the economic crisis has passed, federal financial support for these job-creating projects can be cut back to normal levels, as budgetary discipline is reestablished.

Progressives reject the notion that there is an inherent and inevitable conflict between economic efficiency and social justice. A society that distributes its economic product equitably through a combination of market processes and democratic political choices is certain to be less Hobbesian ("kinder and gentler," according to President Bush) than one that relies primarily on market behavior. Such a society is likely in the long run to be politically more stable and provide a larger domestic market for its output, thus becoming more efficient and more competitive economically. No healthy society can afford to entrust its future to the self-interested calculations of the few hundred unaccountable megaenterprises that dominate today's global markets. The American people continue to look to the federal government to safeguard national security and promote the public interest, as well as to stimulate economic productivity; the reconciliation of these goals is the substance of democratic political choice.

Personal and Family Security

One of the sharpest, most consistent, and most principled divisions between progressives and the Republican right centers on the theme of personal and family security. Though it is no longer fashionable to argue for a welfare state, and though complete economic security can never be achieved, the underlying commitment of progressives is to a government that accepts responsibility for assuring minimal levels of livelihood for citizens as they encounter exigencies that are beyond their individual control, mainly disability, unemployment, old age, and serious illness. They may disagree on the method of financing such programs, on the levels of protection that are feasible and affordable, and on the methods of deterring and countering abuses by health providers and by irresponsible members of the public.

Rightists, despite their highly touted concern for family values, reject in principle this role for government. They believe that the market is the fairest and most efficient allocator of income and that individuals should be held personally responsible to provide for their needs, failing which they should fall back on their families or on private charity (President Bush's "thousand points of light"), but not on government "largesse." Only the most obviously unemployable should be eligible for government assistance. Their particular target has been "welfare" (aid to families with dependent children), the highly unpopular program that appeared to encourage idleness among women and to reward immoral behavior (having children out of wedlock).[14] As this program was cut back sharply in 1996 in favor of "workfare," with uncertain consequences for former welfare clients and their children, this issue is no longer available to Republicans.

In reluctant deference to widespread public support for existing entitlement programs, Republicans pledge not to interfere with federal Social Security (old age and survivors' insurance), and they promise to continue medical care to the elderly (Medicare), but they do so with evident lack of enthusiasm. (They were willing to see their cherished balanced budget amendment fail in the Senate in 1995, rather than accept a provision that would prevent drawing on the Social Security trust fund to balance the budget!) They propose to privatize Social Security and Medicare by creating individual accounts that individuals would be responsible for investing in the securities markets. While this might over the long run provide higher yields than investments in government bonds, retirement annuities would vary with each individual's investment judgment and the vagaries of the securities markets. It would convert Social Security and Medicare from insurance systems with guaranteed and predictable income flows to a lottery from which some might profit while others would be condemned to impoverished old age.

The progressive agenda must address uncertainties surrounding current arrangements for hospital and health care and, for a significant minority, the absence of any coverage at all (see chapter 4). The most sensible and efficient solution would be a universal single-payer system sponsored by the federal government and administered by the federal government and the states. If this system should prove impossible to enact, measures must be taken to shore up the present chaotic and inefficient arrangements so that patients cannot be arbitrarily dropped from the rolls or deprived of needed services by HMOs or insurance companies. Methods must be found to ensure that low-income working families and the self-employed can qualify for affordable health and hospital insurance and that the cost of prescription drugs is covered for Medicare beneficiaries. As in other industrialized countries, paid maternity leave should be mandated for prenatal and postnatal care;[15] competent, safe, and affordable day care should be available to working parents. These measures would go a long way toward safeguarding family security.

There can be no guarantee of employment security in a technologically dynamic, global economy. Nevertheless, a commitment by the federal government to a full-employment strategy, as discussed earlier in this chapter, can be implemented by a policy of economic expansion that continues to create job opportunities, supplemented by an aggressive program of transitional retraining and placement services to parallel the present system of unemployment compensation.

Another dimension of personal security is government surveillence of the safety of products that may be legally marketed in the United States. This is notably the case with pharmaceuticals that are strictly regulated by the Food and Drug Administration. It applies also to a wide range of manufactured products, from baby blankets to lawn mowers and detergents, that are regulated by the Consumer Products Safety Commission. Most Democrats have felt that assuring the public about the safety of products they are urged by advertisers to buy is a proper responsibility of government. This responsibility includes strengthening the ineffectual and outmoded methods of federal meat inspection, improving the inspection of imported fruits and vegetables, and imposing stricter limitations on tobacco advertising and marketing. The Republican right, in response to pressures from some manufacturers have, by contrast, pledged to relax and to cut back many of these protections. The doctrinal divide between the Republican right and progressives is again reflected in their respective approaches to government regulation of product safety.

The Republican right's single positive contribution to the personal security theme responds to a deeply felt public preoccupation with violent crime, along with the fear, anger, and helplessness it engenders among ordinary citizens. Though the incidence of homicides and criminal violence has declined significantly since the mid-1990s, crime remains one of the principal threats to quality of life in the United States. The "conservative" response is more vigorous law enforcement and punishment of offenders, including tougher sentencing, the construction of more prisons, and above all, reinstatement of the death penalty. (Conservatives' patronage of the gun lobby, ironically, sustains the very instrument by which most violent, lethal crimes are committed, including the mowing down of children and teachers on public school premises.) Despite President Clinton's 1994 anti-crime bill, which authorized federal financing for the hiring of 100,000 more police officers and mandated the "three strikes, you're out" policy for the federal courts, many Democrats have been noticeably less enthusiastic about such legislation, concerned that strict enforcement bears most heavily on and discriminates against members of racial minorities. They advocate instead preventive measures which, truth to tell, are as untested for their deterrent quality as the rightist preoccupation with punishment.

Progressives should not be ceding this important dimension of personal and family security to their opponents. The poor, especially inner-city minorities, suffer most from violent crime. Improved economic opportunities are the best form of crime prevention, and it is no accident that the recent decline in violent crime has accompanied improved job opportunities. These positive strides must, however, be complemented by strict measures of deterrence, law enforcement, and gun control combined with greater attention to rehabilitation.[16] By his sponsorship of anti-crime measures, President Clinton has successfully overcome the impression that Democrats are soft on crime.[17]

Equal Opportunity

A component of the American political culture to which conservatives and progressives proclaim equal homage is the principle of equal opportunity for all. Yet, to those differently situated on the political spectrum, it has quite different meanings. To rightists, it means that through diligence and hard work a poor boy may become a prosperous, even a rich man. The poor farm lad, Horatio Alger, or the poor immigrant's son achieving economic success have become the conservatives' version of the "American Dream." To conservatives, government should remain a passive presence in this drama; all depends on individual initiative, drive, hard work, and entrepreneurial vision.[18] For progressives, by contrast, there is much that government can and should do to promote and ensure greater equality of opportunity, not only for the few but for the many. This applies to government at all levels— federal, state, and local.

Perhaps the greatest equalizer is public education. Progressives tend to promote generous financing of public education at all levels, from kindergarten through university, including remedial education for those with physical, mental, or cultural handicaps. Public education in this country faces severe problems and is under siege. Among these problems is the substandard performance, especially by international comparisons, of students at all levels in the basic reading, mathematical, and scientific skills. This problem is exacerbated by gross inequalities in per-pupil spending between and within states. Students from more affluent districts benefit from smaller classes, better qualified teachers, and more modern laboratory and computer facilities.

Because education remains primarily a local function, its financing primarily by property taxes is often a heavy burden on local homeowners. The role of the federal government is necessarily limited. Yet federal funding combined with federal standards can help to improve the supply and the qualifications of teachers, and to provide better physical facilities and pedagogical equipment. The federal courts can intervene to require state governments to meet their constitutional obligation to ensure equal protection of the laws by mandating the equalization of educational funding between richer and poorer districts, in effect shifting some of the burden to state governments. Yet such modest assistance as President Clinton has proposed evoked an angry response from Republicans in Congress as a federal encroachment on states' rights. This response is similar to their passionate rejection, also on states' rights grounds, of Clinton's proposal for national tests of student performance that states might voluntarily adopt to enable parents to evaluate their childrens' schooling by objective standards.

Most distressing has been the concerted Republican attack on public education, a central institution of American democracy. This is expressed in their trashing of teachers' unions and their campaign to privatize education by diverting public funds by voucher arrangements to private schools, including those operated by religious organizations. This innovation is proposed as a way of forcing public schools to compete for students, enhancing parental choice, and improving student performance, even though diverting public funds to sectarian schools violates the constitutional separation of church and state. Thus, instead of seeking innovative ways to improve public schools, the Republican right is pushing measures that would drain resources from public schools and certainly weaken them further.

Much can and must be done by the federal government to realize equal educational opportunities and raise levels of public elementary and secondary schooling. In the pursuit of equal opportunity, progressives should also attempt to ensure that every young man and woman has a chance to pursue postsecondary education, at least through the technical and junior-college levels, with federal financial assistance from scholarships and loans on concessional terms. The federal government should help state and local educational authorities to improve their offerings in adult education, both to help workers up-grade their employment skills and to enable members of the general public to cultivate their leisure-time interests.

Progressives have led the battle for federal legislation that would outlaw and punish discrimination in officeholding, voting, employment, education, housing, and public facilities based on race, ethnicity, lifestyle, or gender. Though these are sometimes violated, notable progress has been achieved in realizing these goals, as registered by the growing presence of women and minorities in institutions and jobs, including some of the more prestigious, from which they had previously been excluded. The widespread practice of racial profiling by law enforcement agencies as well as highly publicized incidents of brutalization of members of racial minorities demonstrate, however, that residual racism persists in this country. Racism from all sources must be combatted, from the Klan and the militias, as well as from the Nation of Islam leader Lewis Farrakhan and his followers.

Government-mandated preferences (e.g., affirmative action) have become a highly contentious issue in American politics and have been losing public support. The Republican right is inclined to scrap such preferences as constituting reverse discrimination against white males, contrary to the American principle of equal treatment of individuals. Democrats tend to support affirmative action as a still-necessary measure, especially to provide a helping hand to members of the large concentrations of African Americans who remain mired in poverty in the central cities and to aspiring African-American entrepreneurs. Progressives have regarded affirmative action as a necessary but temporary set of measures to overcome the legacy of previous patterns of discrimination and exclusion.[19] Until equality of opportunity has been realized for traditionally marginalized categories of Americans, some form of preference, short of quotas and strict proportionality, must be available.[20] The criteria for eligibility should, however, be tightened to exclude those who no longer need such assistance.

Government may contribute to more equal opportunity by supporting public services such as education, job training, agricultural extension, and public libraries that enhance the capacities of individuals to function more productively in the marketplace. And by providing amenities such as playgrounds and cultural events that would otherwise be unavailable in remote communities and low-income neighborhoods. And by facilitating access to clean, safe, and attractive housing for low-income families, including provisions for renters to acquire equity and eventual ownership of their dwellings.

The responsibilities of citizenship in a democratic society should not be confined to participation in the institutions of government. There are numerous opportunities for community service through voluntary associations contributing to religious, charitable, neighborhood improvement, and advocacy activities. These are the institutions of civil society that undergird a healthy democratic polity by providing individuals with experience in self-managed activities, in appreciating societal needs beyond immediate self-interest, and in advocating their values and interests before government. They provide useful intermediation between individual citizens and the state. Progressives believe that government should facilitate and encourage maximum citizen participation in voluntary associations.

Quality of Life

There is much the federal government can do, and has done, to enhance the quality of life for American citizens. Especially notable is the restoration and protection of a clean, healthful, and esthetically attractive physical environment. Dramatic progress has been registered, in this respect, within the living memory of most adult Americans, a feat accomplished not by market forces but by vigorous government initiatives driven by aroused and active citizens' movements. Some of America's most prominent corporations have resisted and continue to resist significant federal initiatives to upgrade the nation's air quality and the purity of its lakes and streams, arguing in favor of market processes or self-regulation, or of devolving this problem to the fifty states. The automobile industry has been a major offender, complaining about and resisting every effort during the past three decades to impose higher safety and emission standards, fearing higher production costs and thus a reduction in either sales or profits. The same applies to the coal-burning electric power industry and to many chemical and paper manufacturers, most of whom soon find that complying with EPA regulations has only a marginal effect on their costs of production and their competitiveness, in large measure because the demand for cleaner production technologies and reduced toxic emissions has stimulated the innovation of new and much more efficient industrial technologies.

The environmental movement has transformed the quality of life in this country. As a boy in Pittsburgh, I remember the days when the city was darkened at noon by heavy smog (fog suffused with soot particles, acids, and other chemical pollutants); when people blew black mucus into their handkerchiefs and housewives washed the interior walls of their houses twice a year to keep them habitable; when recreational activities, such as swimming and fishing in local rivers and streams, were dangerous; when nearby Lake Erie was so filthy with untreated sewage and toxic industrial emissions that fish had disappeared entirely and migratory birds could no longer rest there. All that has changed, all for the better. Much, however, remains to be done to reduce toxic contamination of soils and waterways from chemical fertilizers and pesticides; to reduce fumes from motor vehicles in major urban centers, such as Los Angeles; and, especially, to control the discharge of chloroflurocarbons into the atmosphere at a rate that threatens to deplete the earth's stratospheric ozone layer and produce catastrophic climate changes on this planet. The performance of the U.S. government in declining to conform to the international global consensus arrived at in Kyoto in 1996, which pledged the nations of the world to reduce their emissions in proportion to their current contribution to the problem, is a serious indictment of our national political leadership. This failure was caused by stonewalling by large American corporations, which would be required by these measures to innovate and modify their production technologies. They were supported, as is normal in such cases, by the unilateralist congressional leadership and the disinclination of President Clinton to escalate this issue into a major conflict.

Environmental protection is, thus, a continuing struggle, one in which Progressives have assumed a leading role. The main impulse for progress comes from organized citizen pressure converted by Democratic politicians into government action. Over the years, although a number of corporations have internalized the environmental ethos and proudly practice environmental responsibility, many continue to resist. Conservatives have succeeded in legislating the marketization of pollution rights and interfirm trading of these rights in conformity with standards and goals established for some industries. But the burden of monitoring, compliance, and promoting higher standards remains very much the responsibility of the federal EPA.

Not too many years ago, President Reagan urged the elimination of EPA from the federal government. He was thwarted, however, by the

Democratic majority in Congress. (He then attempted to cripple that agency by emasculating its budget and appointing administrators who opposed environmental regulation in principle!) Today, Republicans tend to support the broad objectives of environmental improvement rhetorically but find reasons to block or delay particular measures, usually at the behest of corporate constituents, property developers, or communities and unions that fear the loss of jobs. Predictably, they embellish this skepticism by the usual invocation of anti-government ideology. The public perception is that Democrats tend to be supportive of environmental initiatives, while Republicans are lukewarm, skeptical, or opposed.[21] The major environmental organizations have, consequently, become constituents of the Democratic Party, whose reputation as environment-friendly is a major political asset, one that candidate Clinton emphasized during the 1996 campaign.

An important contributor to quality of life are civil liberties, the precious heritage of the American nation, especially First Amendment rights: freedom of religion, speech, press, political participation, and organization. Although these rights appear to be secure in late twentieth-century America, the classical warning about vigilance continues to apply. The religious right, firmly aligned with the Republican Party, continues to agitate for school prayer, public observance of religious festivals, the diversion of public funds to sectarian schools, and similar measures that would privilege the status of certain religious denominations while diminishing and even violating the principles and status of others and of non-believers. Progressives must continue their long-standing struggle to maintain the constitutional separation of church and state in order to preserve genuine religious liberty for all.

Perhaps the greatest threat to freedom of expression comes not from government harassment or censorship but from the creeping monopolization of the major media—newspapers, radio, TV, cable, films, and even publishing houses—in the hands of a few large corporate conglomerates. The willingness of the federal government, beginning in the Reagan era, to tolerate such concentration of the information media in so few hands by failing to enforce the anti-monopoly laws (a tendency not reversed, sadly, by the Clinton administration) should be troublesome to progressives, for it handicaps the efforts of original, dissenting, and heterodox thinkers and writers to find public outlets for their views. The unlimited webspace available on the Internet represents a countervailing force, but by no stretch of the imagination can the web compensate for the emergent concentration of ownership and control of the mass media. The ability of a single megacorporation to control the single daily newspaper, a TV outlet, a cable network, and a major radio station in an urban center is a frightening prospect to those who favor free expression of multiple views and perspectives. The time has come for progressives to demand the dissolution of these monopolies.

The decades-long struggle for women to consolidate their victory in the Supreme Court's landmark *Roe v. Wade* decision, which affirmed their right to make their own decisions regarding the responsibilities of childbirth and to terminate unwanted pregnancies legally and safely, has not been conclusively decided.[22] The intractable and frequently violent opposition of the religiously motivated "right to life" movement continues its efforts to reverse *Roe v. Wade*, to criminalize abortion under virtually all circumstances, and to impose their religious principles on the entire nation by government power. This is a major issue not only of quality of life but of human rights as well. Democrats tend to support women's rights to privacy and choice, whereas Republicans are more and more closely aligned with the right to life movement, a price they seem willing to pay for the allegiance of the religious right. This political alignment helps to account for the sharp "gender gap"—a substantial majority of women identifying with Democrats and voting for their candidates. Until a reasonable compromise is found between these sharply conflicting positions, progressives must continue to stand behind this dimension of women's rights.

An important quality-of-life factor is the ability of citizens to enjoy serious informational, educational, and cultural experiences independently of the mass entertainment channels that monopolize time on commercial radio and television. In order to enhance advertising revenues by attracting larger audiences, commercial radio and television stations have converted what they call news broadcasts into a new species of entertainment, "infotainment." One never encounters symphonic or operatic music or observes serious drama on these media, for these are believed not to be of interest to advertisers or mass audiences. Progressives should continue to insist on generous government financing for public radio and TV, similar as they are to the long-standing public financing of libraries and adult education. The efforts of the Republican right to eliminate such federal assistance in 1995 was thwarted by an outpouring of citizen support from all areas of the country. Nevertheless, the level of federal financing was reduced from $370 million in 1993 to $339 million in 1996 and needs to be restored.[23]

The National Endowment for the Arts makes possible modest assistance ($120 million in 1999) to America's creative and performing artists. This funding also brings opera, ballet, drama, classical music, and serious art to communities that would otherwise have no access to live performances, not only small towns in remote areas but also urban neighborhoods whose residents cannot afford the current high costs of serious musical and dramatic performances or shows of original American paintings and sculpture. The extension of these opportunities to ordinary Americans is enabled by this small federal subsidy, which the Republican congressional leadership has been trying to eliminate in part because the NEA has sponsored controversial art. They appear to believe that if serious culture cannot hack it on the commercial markets, it ought to be confined to the few who can afford it or be allowed to die.[24]

An Energetic Foreign Policy

The dimensions of an energetic foreign policy informed by the concept of enlightened self-interest, implemented where possible by the practice of international cooperation, and undergirded by unrivaled economic and military strength have been outlined in chapter 4.[25] In the current interdependent global system, they constitute a major theme in the progressive strategy for the twenty-first century.

The United States has emerged from the Cold War as the world's single superpower, with the capacity to project its military power, if need be, on all continents.[26] With global power comes global responsibilities, to build and defend an international order that greatly benefits the United States and other nations as well—that preserves the peace; facilitates unobstructed commerce in goods, services, and information; and enables all peoples to improve their material living standards, develop their distinctive cultures, and expand the enjoyment of basic human rights. Because America's motives are suspected and its power is resented in elite circles of many countries, power of this magnitude must be employed prudently and where possible cooperatively, disciplined by the principle of enlightened self-interest.[27] Enlightened self-interest implies that the United States, in pursuit of its own objectives, attempts at the same time to accommodate the reasonable objectives of other states and nations and to participate fully in and seek to strengthen the institutions of international cooperation.

The Democratic Party under Presidents Roosevelt and Truman led the United States after World War II away from its traditional isolationism into a posture of international leadership, including the sponsorship of a network of multilateral organizations, such as the United Nations and its specialized agencies (e.g., the World Health Organization and the Food and Agriculture Organization), the International Monetary Fund and the World Bank, and military alliances, such as NATO. For more than four decades, under Republican Presidents Eisenhower, Nixon, Ford, Reagan, and Bush and congressional Republican leaders such as Senators Vandenberg and Dirksen, this consensus became bipartisan. Traces of isolationism persisted on the margins of both parties, anti-imperialism among some post–Vietnam War Democrats, Fortress America wariness of foreign entanglements among some Republicans.

This bipartisan consensus was shattered in the 1990s by Republican congressional leaders who advocate a post–Cold War posture of "unilateralism" in our external relations, the contemporary version of pre–World War II isolationism. The high point of neo-isolationism was the Republican controlled Senate's rejection in October 1999 of the Comprehensive Test Ban Treaty, reversing the bipartisan consensus in favor of limiting nuclear testing by international agreement that had been initiated by President Eisenhower and honored by all his successors. This reckless act eliminates any inhibitions to nuclear weapons testing, thus to nuclear proliferation, by any state. The atmosphere surrounding this vote suggested that, the merits of the treaty aside, the rightist leadership relished the opportunity to humiliate President Clinton.[28]

Progressives should encourage moderate Republicans to join them in restoring the bipartisan consensus on American leadership on behalf of international cooperation. They should continue to insist that, despite our impressive military and economic capabilities, the United States cannot successfully pursue its own national objectives in this interdependent world except by cooperating with other countries. Many matters of direct concern to our people, such as environmental protection, public health, airline safety, economic stability, and international terrorism are regional, even global in scope; these require coordinated action under the auspices of international organizations such as NATO, the United Nations, and the IMF. For example, it is clearly in our interest to prevent the current collapse of several Asian economies and of Russia from precipitating a global recession. The IMF, which draws its resources from all the industrialized countries, has proved to be a useful alternative to direct and very costly U.S. intervention. But we cannot expect the IMF to intervene effectively unless we contribute to increasing its resource base.[29] Likewise, we had much at stake in preventing the crisis in Kosovo from igniting a Balkan war, but neither NATO nor the UN is able to mount an international peacekeeping operation unless we provide our share of financing and manpower. The current wave of neo-isolationism must be vigorously resisted in debate, in principle, and in practice. The prospect of the United States being expelled from the General Assembly of the United Nations for nonpayment of dues is a sobering reminder of the damage inflicted by the recklessness of the present generation of unilateralists and of how closely they resemble the isolationists who prevented the United States from joining the League of Nations three generations ago. "The emerging global order that benefits us more than any other country demands an enforcer. That's America's new burden."[30]

The military is but one, and in most situations, the only ultimate instrument of power and influence. Our economic resources can be deployed to stabilize the international economic order and to help low-income countries overcome ignorance, disease, and poverty in the spirit of President Truman's Point 4 Program of a half century ago. As a great power concerned with promoting more open flows of ideas and information, exchange of persons is a vital, low-cost instrument of foreign policy. Progressives should continue to promote successful programs such as the Peace Corps, which enables young Americans to participate in service roles in low-income countries; the Fulbright programs, which support study and research in overseas educational institutions; and various activities that arrange for short-term exchanges of journalists, public officials, businesspeople, scientists, military personnel, and athletes. In 1996, 454,000 students came to the United States to study at our colleges and universities under the auspices of foundations, charitable organizations, foreign governments, international agencies, or on their own. Nothing contributes more to the extension of U.S. influence of all kinds than these experiences.[31] Given the growing scale and depth of transnational interdependence, commercial and informational as well as political, the limited foreign-language skills of most young Americans and their ignorance of foreign societies and cultures represent a severe handicap. There is much the federal govern-

CHAPTER EIGHT

The Twenty-First-Century
Progressive Majority

Where there no vision the people perish.
—Proverbs 29.18

If we win, we must win because we are progressive.
—Franklin Delano Roosevelt, letter to R. S. Copeland,
February 23, 1931

A successful political movement requires not only a set of themes that excite and reassure a large public but also a combination of tactics and resources that mobilize and sustain political action. The themes that have been outlined in chapters 4 and 5 and elaborated in chapter 7 lay out the elements of an electoral platform that addresses the needs and concerns of the rapidly evolving American nation, and appeals to their image of what Americans should stand for above and beyond immediate self-interest.

Democrats can count on the support of constituencies that represent disadvantaged and less affluent communities, those who favor active government in the interest of social reform, and those who are motivated by social idealism and visions of a better society.

Included in this coalition are members of marginalized minorities whose aspirations for more equitable, non-discriminatory treatment and full inclusion in the opportunities of American life have long been championed by Democrats. Among them are African Americans, homosexuals, recent immigrants including Hispanics, and women.[1] The decided preference of woman voters for Democratic candidates has become a fixture in American politics.[2] The coalition encompasses most government employees, including teachers, as well as environmentalists and persons concerned with the conservation and prudent management of the nation's natural and scenic resources. Though the ranks of organized labor have been depleted in recent years, union members remain one of the core sources of Democratic supporters and activists. Academics, writers, creative and performing artists, and those who value intellectual freedom of expression and artistic experimentation have found themselves more comfortable as members of the Democratic rather than Republican coalition, which preaches traditional morality and conformism.

The Republican right can muster their own impressive coalition: evangelical Christians and moral traditionalists, gun merchants and owners, small businessmen, "developers," large farmers, anti-abortionists, corporate executives, and wealthy rentiers. Since these contending support groups are more or less evenly balanced, the outcomes of elections depend on their respective success in attracting potential supporters to the polls and, above all, in appealing to swing voters.

The choices of swing voters are decisive, since more and more Americans identify themselves as "independent," depending on their assessment of individual candidates and party positions on particular issues.[3] This middle range of uncommitted voters includes the growing cohorts of senior citizens who vote in larger proportions than any other age group. They are cross-pressured between concern to protect their federal entitlements and their inclinations toward moral and fiscal conservatism.[4] Among the swing voters are non-union workers and the rapidly expanding category of professional, technical, and white-collar employees who staff the enterprises of the information age.

An important bellwether is young voters: during the New Deal–Great Society decades, students and other young people tended to express their idealism and to identify with and support Democrats as the agents of modernizing economic, racial, and even international (e.g., Peace Corps) justice, whereas Republicans represented stand-pat conservatism and isolationism. With the Reagan era, young people, now cynical about government and politicians, abandoned idealism in favor of strictly personal goals and materialistic advancement. Republicans seemed more "with it" than the tired old Democrats still running against Herbert Hoover and repeating the shopworn mantras of the 1960s. American youth is a critical constituency that progressives must struggle to reclaim; this helps explain President Clinton's campaign to make higher education available and affordable to all young people who wish to take advantage of it. Young people tend to be tolerant on matters of personal behavior, which ought to ally them with Democrats rather than Republicans, who have become hostages to the moral imperatives of their religious-right constituents.

Progressives have the opportunity to energize this generation of young Americans with a challenge to transcend their preoccupation with material interests and embrace the progressive vision of America. This America is confident of its strength and its values, inclusive of all its citizens, generous to the disadvantaged and to those who have fared less well in life's encounters, insistent on justice and a helping hand to the victims of past and recent discrimination, concerned with protecting the environment and the nation's endowments of natural resources, and committed to international cooperation on behalf of peace, environmental improvement, and assistance to the poorer nations in their struggles against poverty, ignorance, and disease. This is the contemporary version of the "improving society," which, as I mentioned in chapter 2, has been one of the important, continuing strands of American culture.

Similar challenges, when launched in their time by Presidents Lincoln, Theodore Roosevelt, FDR, and Kennedy had been enthusiastically received by their generations of American youth. They, too, had become jaded, disgusted, and turned off by the sharp practices, the odor of moral corruption, the mean-spirited bickering, and the cynical interest-mongering that characterized public affairs in their day. Their enthusiasm for a more meaningful style of politics and for bringing American practices more closely in line with the enduring values of American civilization transformed their political environment; their idealism contributed to the political and social reforms of the progressive era, the New Deal, and the Great Society. To raise their moral vision above the level of self-absorbed individualism, to recognize that no person is an island, that the well-being of each depends on the health of the whole, to overcome the prevailing cynical attitude toward public affairs, to universalize participation in the American dream—this is the challenge that progressives can offer to the oncoming cohorts of America's youth. This vision and these expectations require an expansion in the public sphere and a commitment to participate actively in public affairs.

In July 1999, President Clinton visited several of the most poverty-stricken areas of the country in order to call attention to the persistence of extreme poverty in this era of prosperity. These sites included the Oglala Sioux reservation at Pine Ridge, South Dakota, where the rate of unemployment is estimated at 75 percent and most of the residents subsist in crowded hovels unfit for human habitation. Although his compassion was genuine, all that President Clinton felt able to offer these poorest of America's poor was tax concessions that might encourage private enterprise to set up operations at Pine Ridge. But this is little more than the failed Republican idea of "enterprise zones" in the central cities. Far more is needed in education, housing, and job creation before a viable private economy can emerge in the Pine Ridges of this country. Such services are readily affordable in an economy that projects hundreds of billions in revenue surpluses. But Clinton, falsely accused by his enemies of extending the reach of the state, has, in truth, accommodated to the prevailing neo-liberal dogma of small government.

Progressives must encourage their Democratic allies to reassess the resources and capabilities of the federal government, acting alone or in partnership with citizens' associations, the states, and private enterprise, for addressing America's unsolved problems, such as extreme poverty among the Oglala Sioux, the yawning trade deficit, health care for the uninsured, and substandard educational performance. Government alone cannot solve every problem, but neither should its hands be tied in deference to rightist ideology.

Democrats must stop downplaying the role of government, a tactic that stamps them as pale and unconvincing shadows of the Republican right. They must be willing to argue—and to present evidence in the spirit of their predecessors—that an energetic federal government, as their common instrument, has the capacity to effectively address the problems of security, opportunity, and quality of life that confront most Americans in their everyday lives, thereby mitigating the harsher consequences of dynamic capitalism. Measures that have been listed in chapter 4 as irreducible functions of the federal government—all of which depend on governmental initiatives—can help to relieve the anxieties of the middle classes and the working poor over their future and the prospects for their children. But necessary as these measures are, they are not sufficient.

Democrats must be willing to go beyond the minimum. They must combat at the intellectual level the tattered notion that government dare not "interfere" in the operations of the economy, no matter how serious the problem. The historical record in this country teaches just the opposite. Beginning with Hamilton's 1791 *Report on Manufactures*, many of the outstanding successes in our economic history have resulted from active initiatives by the federal government, in no case displacing private enterprise but supporting and stimulating its performance. The method may be direct intervention, for example, the network of public services and regulations combined with supportive programs by state governments and farmer organizations that have yielded the most productive agriculture in the world; or massive federal subsidies such as land grants, which financed railroad construction, at that time the largest U.S. industry, during the last third of the nineteenth century; or tax subsidies, such as the exemption of home mortgage interest from federal income taxation, which has stimulated home construction and home ownership; or direct regulation, such as patent protection, which has facilitated the commercialization of major industrial innovations; or divestitures by government to U.S. corporations at bargain rates of modern industrial plants financed by government during World War II; or large-scale procurement activities, such as military contracting, which have nursed major industries from commercial aircraft to computers; or the post–World War II GI Bill of Rights, which enabled millions of returning veterans to upgrade their skills for civilian employment, gave them access to college education, and facilitated home ownership by providing federal guarantees for low-interest mortgages. The human genome project, the scientific core of the burgeoning biotechnology industry, and the Internet were initiated by the federal government. The federal government has historically been a major force in the development of the American economy. Where today's needs or future opportunities require, these ample precedents should apply.

Although much progress has been registered in recent years, race relations remain our principal unsolved problem. The same formula of tolerance and acceptance of social pluralism that has enabled the American commonwealth, with its dynamic and ever-evolving diversity of religious creeds and ethnic communities, to survive and prosper in peace and mutual respect must be extended to race relations and remain a core principle of the progressive ethos and of its electoral strategy.[5] This strategy of inclusiveness has mandated the strict separation of church and state in order to protect freedom of conscience and of organization for believers and non-believers alike, and respect for the right of privacy, the right to be left alone in matters of personal behavior, including sexual lifestyle and reproductive choice—neither of which infringe on the equal rights of others. Progressives must continue to vindicate the principles of freedom of belief, freedom of expression, and the right to be free of government supervision in matters of nonviolent and non-coercive personal deportment. The periodic outcroppings of coercive religious fundamentalism and moral absolutism, which have emerged as a component of the Republican right, must continue, in the Jeffersonian tradition, to be vigorously resisted by succeeding generations of progressives.

Progressives must relearn the arts of political mobilization at the grass roots. Republicans will continue indefinitely to raise and spend substantially more campaign money than Democrats, permitting them to purchase more TV time and finance more direct mailing and telephoning, while resisting any limitations on expenditures or requirements that TV and radio stations be compelled to offer free time to competing candidates. The only way Democrats can compensate for these built-in financial handicaps is to outperform Republicans at the grassroots, a contest they have been losing in recent years because of their inability to match the zealous energies of members of the Christian coalition.[6] Democrats must do a better job of organizing, campaigning, and turning out sympathizers at the precinct level by activating their allies and associates in the women's and environmental movements, among ethnic and racial minorities, and among idealistic students and other young people; they cannot continue to rely solely on labor unions, which have sustained much of the brunt of local activism in recent years. By involving members of these constituencies in active politics, progressives can also promote the flow of attractive youthful candidates to compete with younger Republicans. It is important that Democrats mobilize potential voters in low-income neighborhoods, where turnout has been very low. With their many needs for assistance with housing, health, employment, child care for working parents, and education, low-income families stand to benefit greatly from responsive public services that only active government can provide. When they vote, members of minority groups and other low-income individuals normally support progressive causes and Democratic candidates. This is a constituency whose voting participation in substantial numbers can help swing national and state-wide elections in favor of Democratic candidates.[7]

National campaigns in the United States rely much less than in the past on party organization and more on centralized fund-raising, the selection of themes and sound bites from close-support polling, focused mailings and telephoning, and TV messages. Democrats too have learned to play this expensive game of voter manipulation but with fewer resources than their opponents. Both camps also strive to activate their natural support groups at the grass roots, as the American propensity to associate in membership organizations has survived the era of centralized political campaigns. To spread their message and bring supporters to the polls, Democrats and their progressive allies must invest more efficiently than their better-financed opponents in capitalizing on their natural advantage with sympathetic voluntary organizations. This is a task to which the newly aroused cohort of young progressives should address their energies.

The Internet is a low-cost resource that Democrats should begin to exploit in order to spread their message, compensating in some measure for the Republican ability to outspend them on TV. Since young people in large numbers routinely surf the Internet, it is an excellent channel for reaching that vital constituency at a small fraction of the cost of TV broadcasts. Unlike TV, which seeks to manipulate its passive audiences, the Internet is an interactive medium that enables its users to participate in exchanges of opinion. As well as promoting progressive candidates and issues, the Internet can supplant some of the expensive polling that has become a staple of contemporary campaigns.

Regaining majority status and winning national elections will be no simple task for progressives and their allies. Republicans can be counted on to exploit to the fullest their substantial advantage in fundraising. They are likely to retain their electoral majorities in underpopulated Great Plains and Rocky Mountain states, where the dominant interest is the right to exploit natural resources—land, forests, and minerals—untrammelled by government regulation; and in the industrializing Sun Belt, where white males continue to identify with rightist themes by substantial majorities. As long as the post–Cold War prosperity continues, incumbent officeholders of both parties benefit, reenforcing Republican control of the U.S. Senate and their ability to cling to their slender lead in the House of Representatives. (Progressives require a Democratic majority of about thirty in the House to compensate for conservative Democrats, who vote frequently with Republicans on fiscal and social issues.)

The global romance with free market capitalism and diminished government reenforces the standard Republican-rightist hostility to activist government at the expense of progressive initiatives. It is impossible to predict the short-term electoral consequences of extraneous factors such as President Clinton's extramarital flirtations and deceptions and the consequent impeachment proceedings; there can be no guarantee that Republicans will continue to blunder so disastrously as when they closed down the federal government in 1996 and nominated such an unappealing presidential slate that same year; nor can voter reaction to individual candidates in future elections be predicted.

Yet, the outlook for progressives is by no means bleak. Historically, progressives have been called upon to rescue the country from economic recessions, and activist government has proved necessary to mobilize the nation's resources in time of war. After prolonged periods of passive government, societal needs that have been swept under the carpet in the euphoria of prosperity or have been unattended to as contrary to the principle of laissez-faire and minimal government begin to accumulate. Such a period has arrived in the United States after more than two decades of doctrinaire rejection of "big government" by both Republican and Democratic presidents. That during this era of prosperity more than 44 million American citizens should have no guaranteed access to health care, while medical education is being cut back, hospitals are closing, doctors are underemployed, and infant mortality remains the highest among industrialized nations is a national disgrace in this wealthy nation, a scandal that cannot much longer be tolerated or evaded.[8]

That one child in five should be raised in poverty—more than in any other industrialized country— is a damning indictment of the failure of public policy and of the moral bankruptcy of the rightist doctrine of social Darwinism. Or that 10 million Americans do not have enough to eat while eligibility for food stamps is being curtailed.[9] Or that millions of children should be schooled in dilapidated structures in overcrowded classrooms with inadequate textbooks, untrained teachers, and outdated instructional methods. Or that schoolchildren should have unimpeded access to automatic firearms that they can turn on family members and schoolmates with lethal effect. Or that working families should be unable to find decent, affordable housing or competent day care for their children. Or that millions of full-time working men and women should be forced to endure the chronic insecurity of temporary status so that employers, including some major, highly profitable corporations, can evade the responsibility of providing health care and retirement benefits bespeaks a mounting failure of social policy. As real wages for working families lag behind productivity growth, executive compensation escalates, the stock market booms, income disparities between the top 5 percent of income earners and the bottom 60 percent reach all-time highs, and rightists continue to press for lower taxes on high incomes, inheritances, and capital gains.

The neglect of such abuses and unmet needs eventually draws the attention of opinion leaders—novelists, playwrights, artists, social critics, clergymen, and prominent press and radio-TV journalists. Soon thereafter, these themes are taken up by the popular media and galvanized into political action by ambitious politicians. The ethos of self-absorbed consumerism and cynical detachment from public affairs begins to lose its appeal as more and more people tire of its moral emptiness and search for greater meaning in their lives. Many find that meaning in the public sphere, in cleansing the moral corruption in politics (campaign finance reform), in renewed concern for the plight of fellow citizens, and in mitigating or eliminating the political and social abuses that they hold responsible for needless injustice and human suffering. This process explains the triumph of American progressivism in the early years of the current century. One can reasonably anticipate that the early years of the twenty-first century will witness a similar cycle of social reform.

During the last quarter of the twentieth century, while their movement and their values have been on the defensive, progressives needed to be reminded how much closer they are than their rightist opponents to a defining, optimistic theme in the American experience. By deliberate common efforts, through voluntary associations and through democratic government, men and women can help to shape their common future. They need not passively submit to impersonal cosmic forces, such as market processes, when these threaten needless distress; nor be deterred by the pessimistic "law" of unintended consequences from experiments designed to enhance their mutual security, improve the quality of their lives, or promote their economic productivity. The market-based fatalism preached by the Republican right recalls the helplessness of the ancients in a universe dominated by the caprice of the gods whose intentions could be revealed by consulting the oracles (today's stockmarket gurus on TV talk shows), or by reading the tea leaves (today's economic indicators), but could not be influenced by human intervention, which the gods invariably punish as presumption (today's "unintended consequences").

The progressive tradition respects the utility of market processes for efficient resource allocation and celebrates their successes in creating wealth, commercializing technological innovations, and expanding consumer choice, but it does not regard markets as objects of worship. Progressives would not undertake to plan or administer the national economy just as they would not stand by helplessly in the face of remediable suffering, abuses, or market failures. Their confidence in activist government is tempered by their understanding of the limitations of human knowledge and the corruptibility of power. At the same time, their confidence is guided by their belief that problems can be solved by the mobilization of society's resources, including government, and the application of human intelligence; and by the conviction that all Americans are entitled to share in the benefits and responsibilities of the American dream. The latter requires more equitable distribution of the fruits of economic expansion than those produced by unaided market outcomes.

The essence of the American progressives' message is not limited to correcting past failures in public policy or to compensating for neglect and unfairness produced by unregulated markets. It is inspired by the vision of a dynamic nation built on the values of inclusiveness, solidarity, and personal responsibility within the framework of individual liberty. Contrary to the self-interested individualism that has been preached and practiced during the past quarter century, the progressive vision for America emphasizes the responsibility of every American of all backgrounds for their common welfare and their common destiny ("ask not what your country can do for you, but . . ."). It associates optimism and idealism with hard-headed concern for the practical steps that combine economic expansion with family security, individual opportunity, quality of life, and equitable sharing of the fruits of material progress.

The progressive vision is future-oriented, animated by the confidence rooted in America's earliest settlements that ours must be a society whose flaws can be mended by the initiatives of determined citizens and whose reality can increasingly be brought into line with its ideals. Even more than the specific planks of its platform, more than its appeal to particular constituencies, the progressive vision for America can be counted on to inspire a fresh awakening, especially among the nation's youth, to the potentialities of the American dream for all the citizens of this republic.

Every movement for social progress in the American experience has been built on partnerships between determined citizens' organizations and a federal government that eventually responded to their demands. This applied, inter alia, to movements to abolish slavery, enfranchise women, conserve natural resources and protect the environment, extend and enforce civil rights, guarantee collective bargaining for unionized workers, establish Social Security and Medicare for senior citizens, and outlaw discrimination in education, housing, and employment against women, racial minorities, and homosexuals. Progressives must operate through grassroots organizations, in electoral competition, and through government to protect the gains that have already been realized and those that have yet to be achieved, such as universal health care, maternity leave and day care for working parents, effective regulation of lethal weapons, a living wage for full-time workers, adequate schooling for children of all backgrounds, and affordable, post-secondary education for all young Americans. All of these goals require sustained pressure by citizens' organizations and active initiatives by the federal government.

The progressive platform responds to most of the "hot button" concerns of American voters. These concerns include protection of their health benefits from shortchanging by insurance companies and health maintenance organizations (a patients' "bill of rights"); federal assistance to public schools to overcome the shortage of teachers, improve physical facilities, and raise achievement levels; gun control measures to reduce criminal violence; campaign finance reform to redeem the integrity of elections; and legislation to compel cigarette manufacturers to cease promotional advertising to teenagers and to compensate states for the costs of medical and hospital care for persons afflicted with life-threatening diseases resulting from nicotine addiction. On all such matters, the rightist congressional leadership has blocked legislation or watered down proposed action to a point that destroys its effectiveness. Similar efforts to undermine environmental protection have not escaped public attention. On these and other issues, such as the protection of Social Security and Medicare, progressives are well positioned to outcompete the Republican right, whose major appeal is tax reduction. This remains a formidable weapon, but tax reduction is a much lower priority for most Americans—especially if its incidence favors the wealthy few—than the issues cited earlier in this paragraph.

Even though they remain united in their common hostility to government and their affinity for lower taxes, the Republican-right coalition encounters increasing internal strains that threaten to erode their morale and their support base. The most serious is the tension between the Christian coalition and the Republican pragmatists. The former are disillusioned by their inability to impose their agenda on American society by political means, the latter increasingly persuaded that active promotion of that agenda exacts unacceptable electoral costs for Republican candidates. As a result, a large number of evangelicals may choose to forswear political action and revert to their traditional passive avoidance of politics, focusing instead on personal salvation. This development would deprive the Republican-right coalition of a very important constituency of grassroots activists.

Meanwhile, President Clinton's initiatives have helped to relieve Democrats of the demons of fiscal profligacy, softness on crime, and tolerance of welfare abuses that had hobbled their image among large numbers of voters. This correction protected their right flank against attack on these and similar issues and opened political space and opportunity to promote progressive themes that have been in eclipse during the recent cycle of anti-government sentiment. These themes have the potential to renew interest in electoral participation and stimulate turnout among recently abstaining voters, as well as to reverse the abysmally low turnout rates that have characterized recent elections.

All these measures—as well as such unfelt needs as staunching the unsustainable trade deficit—require active initiatives by the federal government, with participation in many cases by state and local governments, business enterprises, and voluntary agencies. No such measures will be enacted, however, without resistance by rightist forces, but the public mood is increasingly receptive to and inclined to demand them. Sensing this trend in public opinion, the Republican presidential front-runner, Governor George W. Bush, reprimanded his party's congressional leadership for their insensitivity to social issues, their opposition to federal aid for education, and their hostility to government: "Too often my party has confused the need for limited government with a disdain for government itself." [10] The auguries for a renewal of progressive political action are more favorable than at any time since President Johnson's War on Poverty thirty-five years ago.

Voting behavior is, of course, determined by factors other than and in addition to the socioeconomic preferences that I have emphasized in this book. These factors may include ethnic and racial affinities or antipathies, beliefs and values (such as the gun culture or sympathy for the underdog), the attractiveness or repugnance of particular candidates, their posture or performance on foreign policy, and voters' generalized sense of well-being or uncertainty about the present or the future. Though President Clinton's sexual philandering and clumsy efforts at evasion and denial involved behavior that was essentially private and fell far short of impeachable offenses, they were more than sufficient to expose him to relentless attack by his political enemies bent on humiliating him personally, destroying his presidency, and driving him from office. Aside from its damage to his reputation, this episode demeaned his high office and further impaired public respect for government, politics, and officeholders.[11] Yet, the political consequences confounded most of the experts. Two-thirds of the public, while condemning Clinton's personal behavior, blamed the Republican right for attempting to impose their own moral and political agenda on the nation for partisan advantage and to drive from office a popular president whom they believe is performing well. Rightists, in frustration, have been reduced to replying with jeremiads condemning the present state of American culture. The backlash may damage Republicans, reenforcing their image as extremists, and provide an unexpected electoral bonanza to Democrats.

Such short-term speculations are less important, however, than longer-term trends. The historical sequence of cycles of activist and passive governments will persist. Activist government, as outlined in chapters 4 and 5, will be indispensable to meeting the social and economic challenges of the early twenty-first century. Because of a quarter century's accumulation of unattended needs—even if no national security or economic emergency should intervene—the time is ripe for a shift in the national mood and public expectations. A few straws in the wind: Clinton has forced the Republican congressional leadership to agree to commit a substantial portion of the impending budget surpluses to strengthening the Social Security and Medicare trust funds and to support public education, rather than to finance tax cuts; a significant minority of the Republican House caucus revolted against the anti-environmental extremism of their leadership and insisted that their party respond to public clamor with legislation to protect subscribers from the sharp practices of HMOs. Republicans and Democrats alike were surprised by the staunch public support for the striking United Parcel Service drivers, which compelled an anti-union management to settle on terms favorable to the drivers.

The early decades of the twenty-first century will witness the fulfillment of globalization; the transnational movement of information, entertainment, capital, goods and services; and to a lesser extent, labor. Apostles of globalization are dismissive of national borders and contemptuous of governments that continue to exercise varying degrees of authority over territorially defined constituents. The global rationalization of economic activity produces many opportunities and benefits for many Americans; but for many others, it exacts pain and entails abuses. To mitigate the pain inflicted by global competition on workers, communities, and small businesses, and to protect them from similar abuses in the future, Americans, like their counterparts in other countries, turn to their governments. Since the logic of globalization as embodied in the doctrine of free trade is not a natural right of transnational enterprises, the federal government must continue to use its countervailing power to regulate practices and provide services that protect American society, even when they constrain the profitability and freedom of action of such firms. When the gaping trade deficit threatens the stability of our economy, government cannot afford to stand aside and wait for the crisis to strike. While recognizing its many benefits, progressives are increasingly wary of globalization. They are unwilling to see government abdicate its responsibilities or be deterred by the bogey of "protectionism" when widespread pain and manifest abuses call for intervention.

Before progressives can expect to capitalize on the opportunities provided by a changing national mood, before they can mobilize those sentiments for political action, there is much work to be done—the work of scholars and publicists.

A convincing rationale for the progressive outlook on public affairs, including the necessity of activist government for the further pursuit of the American dream, must be designed and argued, again and again, in repeated variations on the same basic themes through multiple channels of public expression for multiple audiences. These themes must emphasize (1) the inability of laissez-faire globalism to meet the reasonable needs and expectations of twenty-first-century Americans for increased security and improved quality of life; and (2) the availability of government as their common resource to close the gap between existing reality and their reasonable expectations. Just as the intellectual right, through patient repetition and diffusion of a few basic themes, paved the way for the rightist reaction, which finally triumphed when their time was ripe, a similar course must be followed by their progressive opponents.

Fortunately, they need not wait as long as the rightists were compelled to wait for their hour to come. There are numerous portents that after three decades of celebrating minimal government, that cycle in American experience has about run its course and is coming to an end. The public mood is shifting; the nation is poised for a progressive renewal, for a reaffirmation of the American dream, and acceptance of the federal government as a necesssary agent in its realization. The aim of this book has been to contribute to the intellectual groundwork for that renewal.

NOTES

CHAPTER 1

1. Writing in 1965, Samuel Eliot Morison concluded that under FDR, "the thesis that the federal government is ultimately responsible for the peoples' welfare, employment, and security became generally accepted. Laissez faire . . . gave way to a realization that the state was a natural medium for man's self-expression. . . . Only a federal government over a large area could reconcile conflicting economic interests and subordinate private to public welfare" (*Oxford History of the American People* [New York: Oxford University Press, 1965], 986–87).

2. *The Gallup Poll, 1995* (Wilmington, Del.: Scholarly Resources, Inc., 1996), 251.

3. Council for Excellence in Government, "America Unplugged—Citizens and Their Government," reported in *New York Times*, August 26, 1999, A17.

4. "A Look at the Beliefs in Government Study," *PS:Political Science and Politics* 29, no. 2 (June 1996): 227.

5. Newt Gingrich, *Window of Opportunity: A Blueprint for the Future* (New York: Tom Doherty Associates, 1984).

6. As of March 31, 1999. UN data reported by Global Policy Forum, New York.

7. U.S. Census Bureau, *Statistical Abstract of the United States, 1997*, 117th ed. (Washington, D.C.: U.S. Government Printing Office), 299 (hereafter referred to as *Statistical Abstract*).

8. *New York Times*, January 24, 1996, A1. Some observers believe that Clinton agreed to budget balancing and to cutting back some programs such as welfare—and thus to a more modest role for the federal government—to save the government from its excesses so that it can continue on a more limited scale to be an effective force in American life (Jacob Weisberg, "The Governor-President, Bill Clinton," *New York Times Magazine*, January 17, 1999, 30ff).

9. There have been a few prominent exceptions clustered about such low-circulation journals as the bimonthly *American Prospect* and *Dissent*.

10. The moderates, mostly from the Northeast, accept sexual equality and abortion rights and are comfortable with civil rights for immigrants and racial minorities. They favor limited government and low tax rates but recognize the need for some forms of government regulation and for some social and environmental programs. Though they are prominent among Republican state governors, they represent a diminishing force in the national Republican Party and are virtually unrepresented in its congressional leadership.

11. During the six prosperous years of the mid-1990s, from 1992–97, even though unemployment declined, 16.4 million American workers experienced the trauma of downsizing and displacement. The median period of unemployment was 4–6 weeks; new wages averaged 10 percent below former wages (Bureau of Labor Statistics data reported in the *New York Times*, August 20, 1998, D1).

12. Note the passionate denunciation of free trade by the Republican populist Pat Buchanan in *The Great Betrayal: How American Sovereignty and Social Justice Are Being Sacrificed to the Gods of the Global Economy* (Boston: Little, Brown, 1998). Buchanan regards free trade as a conspiracy among international elites who are irreligious, unpatriotic, and unconcerned with the fate of American working people.

13. U.S. Census Bureau, *Statistical Abstract, 1998*, 421.

14. Between 1970 and 1995, the share of national income available to the lowest quintile of Americans fell from 5.4 to 4.4; that of the highest quintile rose from 40.9 to 46.5. All other quintiles except the highest declined. A 1 percent difference in aggregate income for each family amounts to $1,395—a substantial loss for low-income families (*Statistical Abstract 1997*, 410).

15. Richard J. Herrnstein and Charles Murray, *The Bell Curve: Intelligence and Class Structure in American Life* (New York: Free Press, 1994).

16. To the question "Which do you think is more likely to administer social programs efficiently—the Federal government in Washington or the government of your state?," the responses were federal government, 20 percent; state government, 74 percent; same or no opinion, 6 percent (The Gallup Poll 1995 [Wilmington, Del.: *Scholarly Resources*, 1996], 213).

17. The Personal Responsibility and Work Opportunity Reconciliation Act of 1996, PL 104, signed August 22, 1996.

18. On the question of a progressive vision, see Bruce Ackerman, "The Broken Engine of Progressive Politics," *American Prospect* (May–June 1998): 34–43.

19. The dynamism and pervasiveness of voluntary associations and their contribution to vigorous, democratic society were noted in the mid-nineteenth century by Alexis de Tocqueville in his celebrated *Democracy in America* (New Rochelle, N.Y.: Arlington Press, 1966), first published in 1835. Voluntary associations should not, however, be romanticized as paragons of democratic tolerance

and rational discourse. Some, like the Daughters of the American Revolution, are exclusionary; others, like the National Rifle Association, aggressively promote self-serving, anti-social public policies.

20. Examples of inept tactics include refusing to acknowledge the success of the U.S.-led NATO campaign to reverse the ethnic cleansing in Kosovo (dubbed "Clinton's War"); closing down the federal government in 1996 in a failed attempt to impose their budget priorities; and refusing to enact modest gun-control measures after the Littletown, Colorado, massacre in 1999.

21. See, e.g., Robert Putnam, Robert Leonardi, and Raffaella Nanetti, *Making Democracy Work: Civic Traditions in Modern Italy* (Princeton N.J., Princeton University Press, 1993).

22. For a more extended development of this theme, see Milton J. Esman, *Management Dimensions of Development* (West Hartford, Conn.: Kumarian Press, 1991).

23. On countervailing power, first proposed by Progressives at the turn of the twentieth century, see J. K. Galbraith's classic, *American Capitalism: The Concept of Countervailing Power* (Boston: Houghton-Mifflin, 1952).

CHAPTER 2

1. Sidney Blumenthal, *The Rise of the Counter-Establishment: From Conservative Ideology to Political Power* (New York: Times Books, 1986); see also Godfrey Hodgson, *The World Turned Right Side Up: A History of the Conservative Ascendency in America* (Boston, Houghton-Mifflin, 1996).

2. *Washington Post*, December 11, 1997, A27.

3. Neil Sheehan, et al., *The Pentagon Papers*, as published by the *New York Times* (New York: Quadrangle Books, 1971).

4. Karen M. Paget, "Lessons of Right-wing Philanthropy," *The American Prospect*, no. 40 (September–October 1998): 89–95, summarizes the activities and strategy of the rightist intellectual offensive. See also Blumenthal, *Rise of the Counter Establishment*.

5. Daniel Bell, *The End of Ideology* (New York: Free Press, 1962).

6. Richard Hofstadter, *The Age of Reform: From Bryan to FDR* (New York: Knopf, 1955), 300–326; Arthur M. Schlesinger Jr., *The Crisis of the Old Order* (Boston: Houghton-Mifflin, 1957).

7. Recall the Keynesian quip that in the long run we are all dead.

8. Republican-rightist publicists proclaim their passionate commitment to liberty, especially freedom of entrepreneurial effort from government constraints, claiming that such liberty eventually benefits all. They show little concern for some of the consequences of such liberty, among them increasing inequality, pervasive insecurity, widespread deprivation, and deterioration of the natural environment. This is the mirror image of the European socialist sponsorship of social

equality, which succeeded in stifling entrepreneurial incentives and, in the case of the Soviets and their satellites, in suppressing all expressions of human liberty. Progressives aspire to a wholesome balance that retains incentives and rewards for entrepreneurial initiative and risk taking, while protecting the natural environment and ensuring minimal levels of security and dignity for all members of society, if necessary by government action. Classical conservatives, for example, those adhering to the English Burkean tradition and the social doctrine of the Catholic Church, emphasize social solidarity; their ideology is more compatible with the American Progressive vision than with the radical individualism celebrated by the present generation of American "conservatives."

9. Herbert Spencer, *Social Statics* (1851; New York: Augustus M. Kelley Publishers, 1969). For a recent example of social Darwinian logic, see Herrnstein and Murray, *The Bell Curve.*

10. W. B. Allen and Graham Lloyd, *The Essential Federalist* (Lanham, Md.: University Press of America, 1985); Raoul Berger, *Federalism: The Founding Fathers' Design* (Norman, Okla.: University of Oklahoma Press, 1987); Richard S. Williamson, *Reagan's Federalism: His Efforts to Decentralize Government* (Lanham, Md.: University Press of America, 1990).

11. *McCullough v. Maryland,* 4 Wheat 316. This landmark decision in 1819 confirmed the principle of federal supremacy within its allotted range of functions and the doctrine of implied powers under the "necessary and proper" clause of the Constitution.

12. Theodore Lowi has identified three components of the rightist coalition. Faction one, the economic conservatives, are committed to laissez-faire ideology in the economic sphere and are agnostic on questions of personal morality where government should abstain from interference. In concrete terms, this faction includes corporate America, the main source of funding for right-wing causes. The second faction, the patrician conservatives, includes the intellectual leadership of the New Right. They attempt to combine laissez-faire economics with traditional but upper-class morality. They accommodate both establishmentarian Ivy League Christian conservatives with the mostly Jewish neo-conservatives. They are not averse to using the state to enforce some elements of traditional morality.

Faction three are the moral absolutists, evangelical Christians, whose mission is to restore Christian virtue to a nation they believe has strayed dangerously from the path of righteousness. Although they acquiesce in economic laissez-faire, this populist movement would unhesitatingly use the power of the state to enforce their version of true morality. For tactical reasons, they prefer state governments, where their influence can be more effectively felt. Evangelicals provide the political ground troops for the Republican coalition: they can determine outcomes, especially in Republican primaries, and they have achieved a disproportionate role in the Republican congressional leadership. The impeachment of President Clinton was their project, demonstrating their conviction that pursuing the correct moral path is more important than courting political popularity. Like most true believers (those who claim to know what is best for their fellow men), there is a pronounced intolerance of pluralism and an authoritarian strain in their politics.

The task of Republican Party managers is to attempt to manage the tensions between these three components of the coalition. Lowi believes that this coalition contains irreconcilable cleavages and is too unstable to survive. But while they disagree on the role of government in regulating morality, party managers present a united front on reducing government's role in the economy, cutting taxes, and states' rights (Theodore J. Lowi, Preface to *The End of the Republican Era*. [Norman, Okla.: University of Oklahoma Press, 1996], xi–xxv).

13. Contradictions lurk at the ideological level both among rightists and progressives. Rightists bash government, especially in its economic role, while some demand government action to protect traditional morality. Progressives urge government action to regulate economic abuses and provide social services, while suspecting government actions that infringe on individual liberty and personal privacy, e.g., abortion rights.

14. E.g., *Aliens*, written by the political scientist Jodi Dean and published by Cornell University Press (1998), takes seriously the rumors of extraterrestrial invaders.

15. On this theme, see Martha Derthick, "Dilemmas of Scale in American Democracy," *Miller Center Journal*, no. 4 (spring 1997): 9–16.

16. Carl Sandburg, *The People, Yes!* (New York: Harcourt-Brace, 1936).

17. An example of anti-government humor: "And the Lord spoke to Noah and said, 'In six months I'm going to make it rain until the whole earth is covered with water and all the evil people are destroyed. But I want to save a few good people and two of every kind of living thing on the planet. I am commanding you to build an ark.' 'OK,' said Noah, trembling with fear and fumbling with the blueprints.

"Six months passed and the rain began to fall. The Lord saw that Noah was weeping; there was no ark. 'Lord, please forgive me,' begged Noah, 'I did my best but there were big problems. First I had to get a building permit, but my plan did not meet code requirements. So I had to hire an engineer and redraw the plans. Then I got into a big fight over a fire-sprinkler system. Then my neighbor objected, claiming I was violating zoning by building the ark on my front lawn, so I had to get a variance from the planning board. Then I had problems getting enough wood, because there was a ban on cutting trees to save the spotted owl. I had to convince the U.S. Fish and Wildlife Survey that I needed the wood to save the owls. Then the carpenters formed a union and went on strike. I had to negotiate a settlement with the National Labor Relations Board.

" 'Then I started gathering animals and got sued by animal rights groups. They objected to taking only two of each kind. Then the EPA notified me that I could not complete the ark without filing an Environmental Impact Statement on your proposed flood. Then the Army Corps of Engineers demanded a map of the proposed flood plane.'

" 'Right now I'm trying to resolve a complaint from the Equal Employment Opportunity Commission over how many employees I'm supposed to hire. The IRS has seized all my assets, claiming I'm trying to avoid paying taxes by leaving the country. I don't think I can finish the ark for another five years.'

"Suddenly, the skies began to clear and the sun began to shine; a rainbow arched across the sky. Noah looked up and smiled, 'You mean you are not going to destroy the earth,' Noah asked hopefully.

" 'No,' the Lord replied. 'The government already has.' "

18. Victims of paranoia are especially vulnerable to conspiracy theories and are attracted to the anti-government rhetoric of the extreme right. The gunman who killed two police officers at the U.S. Capitol in July 1998 was a certified schizophrenic who hated the federal government because he was certain that they were spying on him and placing landmines on his property. The bible of the racist and anti-Semitic militias is the *Turner Diaries,* written by William Pierce (under the pseudonym Andrew Macdonald) (Hillsboro, W.Va.: National Vanguard Press, 1990). It contains detailed instructions on how to overthrow the U.S. government by force and replace it with an Aryan republic.

19. Daniel J. Boorstin, *The Americans: The National Experience* (New York: Vintage Books, 1965), 43–48.

20. Arthur M. Schlesinger Jr., *The Cycles of American History* (Boston: Houghton-Mifflin, 1986).

CHAPTER 3

1. U.S. defense expenditures in 1998 were $228 billion. For Europe, including Russia, they totaled $220 billion. China's military expenditures are hard to identify and measure in dollar equivalents. They are believed to be less than 2 percent GDP, compared to 3.4 percent for the United States (*Stockholm International Peace Research Institute 1999* [London: Oxford University Press, 1999]).

2. See chapter 2, note 10.

3. Marshall's landmark decision on federal powers is *McCullough v. Maryland* (4 Wheat 316, 1819).

4. Albert Gallatin, *Report on Roads and Canals* (1806).

5. Daniel Boorstin, *The Americans: The National Experience* (New York: Vintage Books, 1965), 420.

6. Though Jackson favored states' rights, he vigorously rejected South Carolina's claim that a state government may disregard (nullify) a duly enacted federal statute.

7. Richard F. Bensel, *Yankee Leviathan: The Origins of Central State Authority in America, 1859–1877* (Cambridge: Cambridge University Press, 1990).

8. Vast areas of the public domain were granted, often in collusion with incompetent and corrupt officials of federal land offices, to land speculators and timber merchants.

9. William F. Swindler, *Court and Constitution in the Twentieth Century: The Old Legality* (New York: Bobbs-Merrill, 1969), esp. 302–63.

10. Theda Scocpol, "America's First Social Security System: The Expansion of Benefits for Civil War Veterans," *Political Science Quarterly* 108, no. 1 (1993):85–116.

11. The intellectual bible of the Progressive movement was Herbert Croly's *The Promise of American Life* (1909; New York: Macmillan, 1945). Croly invented the slogan "Jeffersonian ends by Hamiltonian means" to designate the progressive strategy of employing the resources of the federal government to serve the cause of individual liberty under twentieth-century conditions. Among the classics of the Progressive movement were Ida M. Tarbell, *The History of the Standard Oil Company* (1904; New York: Peter Smith, 1950); Lincoln Steffens, *The Shame of the Cities* (1906; New York: Sagamore Press, 1957); and Upton Sinclair, *The Jungle* (1906; New York: New American Library, 1960).

12. The strain of suspicion, condescension, and dislike of recent immigrants and their strange, un-American ways characterizing many leaders of the Progressive movement was reflected in Theodore Roosevelt's frequent fulminations against hyphenated Americans and pressures for immigrants to "Americanize," that is, to acculturate to the English language and to Anglo-American middle-class values and ways of life.

13. Wilson had proposed that the federal government be reformed after the model of the British Cabinet–parliamentary system, which he admired because it allowed for responsible government under strong executive leadership (Woodrow Wilson, *Cabinet Government in the United States* [Stamford, Conn.: Overbrook Press, 1947], first published as an essay in the August 1879 issue of *International Review*).

14. In his 1928 election campaign, candidate Hoover declared that American capitalism was on the verge of eliminating poverty. He promised "a chicken in every pot and two cars in every garage." But by 1932 he was prophesying that if the Democrats won the election that year, "grass would grow on the streets of a hundred cities, a thousand towns."

15. Precedent for federal action on human rights issues had been established during the Reconstruction era a century earlier, with the enactment of the thirteenth, fourteenth, and fifteenth amendments to the Constitution.

16. Sidney Blumenthal, *The Rise of the Counterestablishment: From Conservative Ideology to Political Power* (New York: Times Books, 1986).

17. Even if he had not weakened his presidency by sexual indiscretions and deceptions, President Clinton, as Chief Executive in relatively quiet, crisis-free

times, would have faced an emboldened Congress determined to assert its powers.

18. Woodrow Wilson, *Congressional Government: A Study in American Politics* (New York: Houghton-Mifflin, 1900).

19. Corporate leadership is strongly committed ideologically to the doctrine of free-market competition and minimal government. Yet, when they are in trouble, as during the Great Depression, corporate leaders do not hesitate to demand assistance from government; a recent example is the federal bailout of the Chrysler Corporation in 1977. The same applies when they have difficulty coping with foreign competition. Large corporations characteristically attempt to minimize competition by monopolistic practices and inter-firm collusion, despite their doctrinal commitment to free competition. While resisting all forms of government regulation, several industries have lobbied for, achieved, and vigorously defended federal subsidies.

CHAPTER 4

1. E.g., because the Immigration and Naturalization Service is critically understaffed, aliens in several large cities are compelled to wait as long as a year for the interviews that entitle them to permanent residency status.

2. In *Federalist* No. 23, Hamilton argued for an "energetic" central government, one of whose main purposes was to shape and conduct an active foreign policy and, if need be, to use military means to promote and defend the economic and security interests of the young nation.

3. Republican control of the U.S. Senate since 1994 provides the most committed unilateralist, Senator Jesse Helms, chairman of the Foreign Relations Committee, with a veto over foreign policy decisions as well as appointments to diplomatic posts. The United States has refused to sign the anti-land mines treaty, the draft treaty for an international criminal court to prosecute war crimes and violations of human rights, and the global warming treaty. In each case, in addition to the unilateralist charge that they compromise U.S. sovereignty, there were determined bureaucratic or business opponents to these treaties. In the absence of presidential leadership and with the intransigence of Senator Helms and his allies, the United States has stood virtually alone against the weight of world opinion, including our principal allies, in rejecting these treaties.

4. Maintaining growth in the U.S. economy is an example of the need for international cooperation. Recognizing that a major contributor to the global depression of the 1930s was the protectionist and competitive devaluation measures by the major powers, including the United States, the authors of the 1944 Bretton Woods agreements believed they were laying the foundations for international economic cooperation by establishing the IMF and the World Bank. In

1959, following the success of the Marshall Plan, they established the Organization for Economic Cooperation and Development (OECD), whose purpose was
to harmonize the economic policies of the major economic powers (the rich man's
club). The G7 summits were inaugurated a decade later to better coordinate the
efforts of the largest economies. The failure of Japan, the second-largest economy, to correct weaknesses in its financial institutions and to expand domestic
demand contributed to prolonging the economic crisis in several Asian countries, the ramifications of which threaten to curb growth in the U.S. economy. The
United States cannot insulate itself from the world economy, and because we
have the largest and strongest economy, international cooperation is not likely
unless we take the lead. Although reasonable people can dispute the effectiveness of the economic model promoted by the IMF for the troubled economies of
Asia, Latin America, and Eastern Europe, the United States can use its considerable influence in the IMF to revise policies that we consider wrong or ineffectual.
In the absence of help from international sources, including the IMF, these
economies will further deteriorate, with negative consequences to economic
well-being in the United States.

The rightist attack on the IMF has a perverse quality, since the IMF has been
promoting on a global scale the free-market practices that are the centerpiece of
Republican domestic economic policy.

5. *Statistical Abstract, 1997*, 10.

6. There is, however, a significant strain of nativist and racist suspicion and
contempt for foreigners, including dark-skinned immigrants who might undermine the white Christian foundations of American society.

7. Projecting current demographic trends, the proportion of Hispanics
would increase from 11.4 in 2000 to 24.5 in 2050; of Asians, from 3.9 in 2000 to 8.2
in 2050 (U.S. Census Bureau, *Statistical Abstract 1998*, 19).

8. For a rigorous treatment of these relationships, see Thomas J. Palley, *Plenty
of Nothing: The Downsizing of the American Dream and the Case for Structural Keynes-
ianism* (Princeton, N.J.: Princeton University Press, 1998).

9. The radio and TV industry has campaigned vigorously and, for the most
part, successfully to avoid federal regulation of their programming and to deal
with their public responsibilities through self-regulation. The result has been the
virtual elimination of educational, public service, and cultural programming in
favor of gratuitous violence, explicit sexuality, tawdry sensationalism, and ram-
pant commercialism; these are believed to maximize audiences and, hence, profitability.

10. Mainline economics is strongly biased in favor of market solutions and
suspicious of administrative regulation as inefficient, cumbersome, and market
distorting. See Alfred Kahn's influential study, *Economics of Regulation: Principles
and Institutions* (New York: Wiley, 1970). Professor Kahn initiated the process of
airline deregulation during the Carter administration. For a brief account of the

regulatory dilemma, see Daniel Yergin and Joseph Stanislaw, *The Commanding Heights* (New York: Simon and Shuster, 1998), 340–56.

11. Donald F. Kettl, *Sharing Power: Public Governance and Private Markets* (Washington, D.C.: Brookings Institution, 1993).

12. Some otherwise very "conservative" Republicans, backed by the construction, automobile, and trucking industries, favor massive federal funding of highway projects. Classified as old-fashioned pork barrel schemes introduced by legislators to satisfy local constituencies, many such projects could not survive standard benefit-cost calculations.

13. In 1995, 35.5 percent of all research and development expenditures in the United States was financed by the federal government, including a very high proportion of basic scientific research (*UNESCO Statistical Year Book, 1997* [Lanham, Md.: Bernan Press, 1997]). In 1994, federal R&D grants to colleges and universities exceeded $11 billion (National Center for Educational Statistics, *Digest of Educational Statistics 1997* [Washington, D.C.: U.S. Department of Education, Office of Educational Research and Improvement, 1997], table 368).

14. This problem is treated extensively in the Urban Institute publication by C. Eugene Steuerle, Edward M. Gramlich, Hugh Heclo, and Demetra Smith Nightingale, *The Government We Deserve: Responsive Democracy and Changing Expectations* (Washington, D.C.: Urban Institute Press, 1998), 131–34.

15. Even in cold financial terms, these enrichment programs are likely to be less costly to taxpayers than the current expedient of high-cost emergency room treatment for children whose illnesses have been neglected until they become critical, as well as the high costs of law enforcement and prison maintenance: "Based on current rates of first incarceration, an estimated 28 percent of black males will enter state or federal prison during their lifetime, compared to 16 percent of Hispanics and 4.4 percent of white males" (U.S. Bureau of Justice Statistics, *Criminal Offenders Statistics, Sourcebook*, 1999).

16. A large-scale tragedy of the latter twentieth century has been the fate of the millions of working Americans, many of them long-service employees, who have been left high and dry as corporations abandon manufacturing facilities entirely or move their operations to low wage locations overseas. Before implementing such drastic and destabilizing measures, employers should be required by law to provide at least sixty days' notice, severance payments based on length of service, and outplacement services. Some companies have done so, but many have not, treating employees as commodities to be discarded when no longer needed, rather than as fellow human beings under stress. Although the Federal Worker Adjustment and Retraining Notification Act (U.S. Code 29, chapter 23) contains some of these provisions, it contains so many loopholes that it has been largely ineffective. Federal and state governments together should enforce rigorous requirements for advance notice of closings, provide more comprehensive job training than has been available and more aggressive placement services; and, where local jobs are not available, interest-free loans to finance the relocation of

families where suitable jobs can be found. These services should be provided for white-collar as well as blue-collar workers.

17. U.S. Census Bureau data reported in the *New York Times*, October 4, 1999, A1. For 1990, the United States spent 12.2 percent of GNP on health; for the UK, it was 6 percent; Japan, 6.7; Germany, 8.8; the Netherlands, 8.4; France, 8.8; and Denmark, 6.7 (OECD, *OECD Health Systems: Facts and Trends, 1960–1991* [Paris-OECD, 1993] 96).

18. In 1990 life expectancy at birth in the United States was 75.9 years; for France, it was 76.4; Japan, 78.6; the Netherlands, 77.2; Canada, 77. Infant mortality in the United States was 9.1 percent, compared with 4.6 for Japan, 7.1 for Germany, 6.8 for Canada, and 6.0 for Sweden (Ibid., 15, 16).

19. Federal assistance to elementary and secondary education preceded the adoption of the Constitution. The Northwest Ordinance of 1787 adopted by the Confederation Congress set aside one section of land (1 square mile) in each 36-square mile township in the Northwest territories (the current states of Ohio, Indiana, Illinois, Michigan, and Wisconsin) to support public schools. From the outset, public education has been one of the foundations of American democracy.

20. A succession of Gallup polls even prior to the Littleton, Colorado, massacre of school children in May 1999 indicated that by more than two thirds, Americans favor stricter gun control: "A *USA Today* / CNN / Gallup poll conducted last month found that 89% expressed support for gun controls. Of the total, 28% favored restrictions such as waiting periods for gun purchases; 37% favored even tighter controls, such as complete bans on handguns or semi-automatic rifles. And 24% favored making all guns illegal, up from 20% just five years ago" (*USA Today*, June 9, 1998).

21. The sole exception is the Republican effort to limit fund-raising by labor unions, a major source of financial support for Democratic candidates. In October 1999 the Senate Republican leadership defeated the McCain–Feingold bill, a modest bipartisan effort to limit soft money expenditures.

22. For a detailed account of the "soft money" problem, see Dan Clawson, Alan Neustadt, and Mark Weller, *Dollars and Votes: How Business Campaign Contributions Subvert Democracy* (Philadelphia: Temple University Press, 1998), 107–38.

23. The unfortunate Supreme Court decision *Buckley v. Valeo* (424 U.S. 1–1976), linking unlimited campaign expenditures with First Amendment rights, complicates efforts to regulate corrupt practices and limit the "soft money" evasions of campaign expenditure laws.

24. The general posture of the diminishing band of Republican moderates.

CHAPTER 5

1. Examples include Westinghouse, for more than a century a centerpiece of Pittsburgh's economy and civic life. In 1997 its management sold off its world-

renowned manufacturing facilities because they were believed not to be yielding a sufficient return on capital, acquired the CBS television and radio network, abandoned its Pittsburgh headquarters and its responsibilities to the Pittsburgh community, and moved its operations to New York. Eastman Kodak, the mainstay of the economy and civic institutions of Rochester, N.Y., beset by severe competition from Fuji, the Japanese firm, has informed the city fathers that they can no longer rely on Eastman to maintain employment levels in Rochester or to underwrite its charitable and civic institutions.

2. K. Deininger and L. Squire, "A New Data Set Measuring Income Inequality," *World Bank Economic Review* 10, no. 3 (1996): 565–91.

3. U.S. Census Bureau, *Statistical Abstract of the US, 1998,* 473.

4. The reality of class as a factor in American society is beyond the scope of this book. It should be noted, however, that levels of family income correlate closely with levels of personal health and longevity and with levels of educational attainment. The latter correlate, in turn, with lifetime earning capacity. The health data are drawn from the Report of the National Center on Health Statistics, August 1998.

5. Data from the U.S. Bureau of Justice Statistics as reported in the *Economist,* March 20, 1999, 30–31.

6. *Statistical Abstract, 1997,* 424. In 1997, for the first time in two decades, real family incomes rose slightly above the 1977 level.

7. *Statistical Abstract, 1997,* 513.

8. The personal savings rate fell below zero during the fourth quarter of 1998; instead of saving, Americans are liquidating their personal savings and spending them. To the extent that the federal government is running fiscal surpluses, government is now contributing to national savings.

9. Labor productivity grew at an annual average of 2.3 percent in the century between 1870–1970 but managed to increase by only 1.1 percent annually during the next quarter century (Richard K. Lester, *The Productivity Edge: How U.S. Industry Is Pointing the Way to a a New Era of Economic Growth* [New York; W.W. Norton, 1998]). Beginning in 1998, productivity began to recover.

10. U.S. Census Bureau data reported in the *New York Times,* October 1, 1999, A20.

11. From 5 million to 5.3 million families during the decade of the 1990s (U.S. Department of Housing and Urban Development, reported in the *New York Times,* April 28, 1998, A14).

12. Data from the U.S. Department of Health and Human Services as reported in the *New York Times,* January 25, 1999, A14.

13. The Nobelist Robert Solow points out that the addition of former welfare clients to the labor markets either lowers current wage rates or displaces existing members of the low-wage labor force. Recent rates of economic growth have not been sufficient to absorb large numbers of unskilled or semi-skilled mostly female workers, unless government is prepared to finance additional public service jobs

oriented especially to ex-welfare women ("Guess Who Pays for Workfare," *New York Review of Books* 45, no. 17 [November 5, 1998]: 36–37).

14. A recent study in New Jersey indicated that two-thirds of those who left welfare in 1997 remain below the federal poverty level and have experienced serious housing problems. A third of those who hold jobs were living below the poverty line (*New York Times*, October 22, 1999, B6). Observers have noted increased pressures on food banks and homeless shelters as ex-welfare recipients have difficulty meeting their basic needs on sub-poverty wages.

15. On cooperative federalism, see David B. Walker, *Toward a Functioning Federalism* (Cambridge, Mass.: Winthrop Publishers, 1981). See also Morton Grodzins, *The American System: A New View of the Government of the United States* (Chicago: Rand-McNally, 1966). Steuerle et al. (see bibliography) briefly outlines a pattern for allocating functions between the federal and state governments (177–81).

16. For example, labor union members in South Carolina and Alabama, Mexican Americans in California, and African Americans in Texas may consider their interests better served by the federal government than by their state governments.

17. Richard S. Williamson, *Reagan's Federalism: His Efforts to Decentralize Government* (Lanham, Md.: University Press of America, 1990).

18. Surveys conducted in 1995 and 1997 by Peter Hart and Robert Teeter for the Council for Excellence in Government, Washington, D.C. revealed a consistent pattern of greater confidence in local and state rather than the federal government. However, "Americans are optimistic that government could be more effective and work better for them, but at present is not living up to their expectations."

19. The Unfunded Mandates Reform Act of 1995 (PL No. 104–4).

20. For example, *United States v. Lopez*, 115 S CT 1624, 1995.

21. Herbert Storing, *What the Anti-Federalists Were For* (Chicago: University of Chicago Press, 1981).

22. Stephen Moore and David Stansel, *How Corporate Welfare Won*, Cato Institute, Policy Analysis No. 254, May 15, 1996.

23. Actual outlays for 1998 reported in U.S. Office of Management and Budget, *Budget of the U.S. Government, Fiscal Year 2000* (Washington, D.C.: U.S. Government Printing Office, 1999).

24. General government current receipts in the United States as a percentage of GDP in 1996 were 31.6 percent. Comparable figures for Germany were 45.3; for France, 50.3; for Britain, 37.2; for the Netherlands, 47.3; for Canada, 42.7; for Japan, 31.7 (*OECD Economic Outlook*, June 1998).

25. The theme of the now-discredited school of supply-side economics that flourished during the Reagan years. It was dubbed by future President Bush as "voodoo economics."

26. Congressionally mandated reforms in 1998 require the IRS to revise its procedures and become more "taxpayer-friendly."

27. Actually, foreign aid and welfare constitute less than 2 percent of the federal budget.

28. Rightist economists argue that reducing taxes on the wealthy stimulates capital formation since upper income people have a high propensity to save and to invest their savings. Yet, after the 1996 reductions of tax rates on capital gains and the stock market boom of the 1990s which expanded the wealth of upper income families, the national savings rate fell to its lowest point ever, turning negative in 1998.

CHAPTER 6

1. David Stockman, *The Triumph of Politics: Why the Reagan Administration Failed* (New York: Harper and Row, 1986), 394, cited by Lowi, *End of the Republican Era*, 93.

2. Harold Lasswell, *Politics: Who Gets What, When, How* (New York: Whittlesey House, 1936).

3. The World Bank, a bastion of economic orthodoxy, after attempting during the 1980s to impose minimal government on a number of low-income countries through "structural adjustment" reforms, finally concluded that good government ("governance," in their language), not minimal government, is the prerequisite to economic stability and expansion. This is the theme of its 1997 World Development Report, *The State in a Changing World* (New York: Oxford University Press, 1997).

4. The simultaneous terrorist bombing of the highly vulnerable American embassy compounds in Kenya and Tanzania in August 1998, with their heavy toll in innocent lives, can be traced to the failure to provide sufficient funds to protect them from such terrorist acts or to construct more secure buildings.

5. Judith Modell, *Town without Steel: Envisioning Homestead* (Pittsburgh: University of Pittsburgh Press, 1998).

6. Instead of a tactic reserved for fundamental issues, the senatorial filibuster has recently become a routine, extraconstitutional abuse by which minorities of two-fifths plus one can block measures favored by the majority, such as campaign finance reform. This abuse can and should be rectified by modifying the Senate's rules of procedure.

7. Woodrow Wilson, *Congressional Government*; Harold J. Laski, "The Parliamentary and the Presidential Systems" *Public Administration Review* 4, no. 4 (autumn 1944): 347–59, hereafter, *PAR*; Donald K. Price, "A Response to Mr. Laski," *PAR* 4, no. 4 (autumn 1944): 360–63; "Toward a More Responsible Two Party System: A Report of the Committee on Political Parties, American Political Science Association," *American Political Science Review*, supplement 44; no. 3 (September 1950).

8. Actually, 49 percent (U.S. Census Bureau, *Statistical Abstract 1998*, 297).

9. 424 U.S. 1.

10. See Margaret Weir and Marshall Ganz, "Reconnecting People and Politics," in Stanley B. Greenberg and Theda Scocpol, eds., *The New Majority: Toward a Popular Progressive Politics* (New Haven: Yale University Press, 1997).

11. The inspiration for this campaign was David Osborne and Ted Gaebler, *Reinventing Government: How the Entreprenurial Spirit Is Transforming the Public Service* (Reading, Mass.: Addison-Wesley Publishing, 1992). Osborne and Victor Colon Rivera have followed with *Reinventing Government: Facilitator Guide and Workbook* (San Francisco: Jossey-Bass, 1998).

12. "Vice President Gore's reinventing government task force—and the book on which it was based—were flawed from the beginning because they ignored the most basic differences between government and business. Like so many other management fixes, Gore's effort merely rearranged the building blocks of bureaucracy while doing nothing to ensure that the the builder had the right construction skills. . . . More than unhelpful, the public sector management fads—from reinventing to reengineering to downsizing—hurt government. They leave government worse off than it was before. For each time some poor public official holds up one of these plans as the magic tonic to save government, people believe. And each time they're disappointed" (Taegan D. Goddard and Christopher Riback, "You Won—Now What," *IPA Report*, New York, Institute of Public Administration [summer 1998]: 3–4).

13. Gerald E. Caiden, *Administrative Reform* (Chicago: Aldine Publishing, 1969); *Administrative Reform Comes of Age* (New York: W. de Gruyter, 1991).

14. The President's Committee on Administrative Management, *Report* submitted to the president and Congress in accordance with PL 739, 74th Congress, second session (Washington, D.C.: U.S. Government Printing Office, 1937); U.S. Commission on Organization of the Executive Branch of the Federal Government (Hoover Commission) *Report* (Washington, D.C.: U.S. Government Printing Office, 1949); Commission on Organization of the Executive Branch of the Government (second Hoover Commission), *Final Report to Congress* (Washington, D.C.: U.S. Government Printing Office, 1955).

15. The adjustment of incentives can have bizarre effects. Under Republican pressure, IRS agents have been advised that they must learn to be customer friendly, that their performance will be judged not by the money they bring in but by their courtesy in treating "customers." After a year of these revised incentives, the management of IRS in 1999 became concerned that the government is losing billions in revenues legally due from taxpayers because its agents have stopped leaning on tax evaders to produce the funds they owe the government. Their inability to collect taxes owed to the government is exacerbated, as noted in chapter 4, by deep cuts in staffing.

16. The federal government invests far more heavily in merit-based selection, training, and equipment for the armed forces than it does for the civilian services.

Such expenditures for the armed services are seldom opposed or begrudged by rightist pundits or politicians. The result is a superbly trained and highly educated officer corps.

17. Mark J. Popovich, ed., *Creating High Performance Government Organizations* (San Francisco: Jossey-Bass, 1988). For a critical evaluation, see Alisdair Roberts, "Performance-Based Organizations: Assessing the Gore Plan," *Public Administration Review* 57, no. 6 (November–December 1997): 465–78.

18. The difficulty of closing redundant military installations and veterans' hospitals in the face of determined local community pressures, employee groups, and congressional footdragging illustrates the limitations of naïve notions of instrumental efficiency in government and of applying business practices to federal operations.

19. "Accountability" and "transparency" have become prominent buzzwords among critics of government operations, assuming that there is normally a deficit of legal and political control of bureaucratic conduct. This charge cannot be sustained in evaluating the federal bureaucracies. In addition to internal departmental controls, external scrutiny is exercised by congressional subcommittees both in annual appropriations reviews and special investigations, and by periodic interventions by individual members of congress; by the courts; by investigative journalists; and by interest groups that weigh in on legislative proposals, administrative regulations, and day-to-day operations. While the armed forces and the intelligence agencies are insulated from some of these controls, civilian agencies are exposed to all these multiple sources of accountability and take them very seriously.

CHAPTER 7

1. The intellectual disarray of the moderate left in the United States is matched by a similar phenomenon in Europe. Though social democratic parties now govern in Britain, France, Germany, and Italy, they have no clear policies that distinguish them from their conservative opponents, whom they displaced mainly because of the latters' failures in office (e.g., corruption and arrogance among British Conservatives, the inability of German and French conservatives to deal with high rates of unemployment). Europeans of the right as well as the left have not indulged, however, in the anti-government rhetoric that has characterized public discourse in the United States.

2. The philosopher, Richard Rorty, chides the intellectuals of the contemporary left for their obsession with cultural, non-economic issues and for their spectatorial pessimism about the capacity of American society and government for reform and self-improvement (*Achieving Our Country: Leftist Thought in 20th Century America* [Cambridge, Mass.: Harvard University Press, 1988]).

3. Ironically, the successes of the Clinton administration in restoring modest economic growth, low unemployment, low inflation, and a balanced federal budget have convinced some Americans that they have little need for government. At the same time, the odor of campaign finance scandals and the media exploitation of Clinton's sexual lapses have further alienated them from politicians and government.

4. During Reagan's presidency, the national debt more than doubled, from $995 billion in 1981 to $2.6 trillion (*Statistical Abstract, 1997,* 372). The annual debt accumulation during these years greatly exceeded the rate of economic growth.

5. During the fall of 1999, congressional Republicans celebrated their latter-day devotion to Social Security by attempting to block the use of any Social Security payroll tax revenues for federal programs other than Social Security, an abrupt departure from precedent. Their transparent purpose was to promote their goal of minimal government by blocking the use of any of the budget surplus, as President Clinton had proposed, to meet urgent needs for education, health care, and environmental protection.

6. This phenomenon is known as "bracket creep."

7. For data on consumer debt, refer to note 7, chapter 5. In the event of economic recession, many borrowers will be unable to service their consumer debt, leading to large-scale personal bankruptcies and home mortgage foreclosures and threatening the solvency of financial institutions. Should that credit bubble be pierced, confidence in the economy would be shaken, triggering an economic recession.

8. During this period the percentage of aggregate income received by the lowest quintile fell from 5.3 in 1981 to 4.2 in 1993; the second quintile fell from 11.4 to 9.9; the highest quintile rose from 41.2 to 47, and the top 5 percent increased from 14.4 to 20.3 (*1997 Statistical Abstract,* 470).

9. U.S. Census Bureau, *Statistical Abstract, 1998,* 438.

10. Some high-school graduates could qualify for higher-skill service jobs that expand with the growing information-age economy. Those who must find employment in low-skill service jobs need to be protected by minimum wages, assured medical and health services, reliable day care, and subsidized low-income housing so that they can provide adequately for their families.

11. Between 1978 and 1994, the real wages of high school graduates, representing 40 percent of the labor force, declined by 11 percent (data from *Monthly Labor Review,* July 1997, 3–14).

12. Corporate CEOs in 1998 were paid 326 times the average earnings of factory workers, up from 44 in 1960. Yet, managers feel sorry for themselves because they are overworked and insecure. They have too little time for their families and for personal recreation and fear that they may be arbitrarily dismissed at any time (data reported in the *Economist,* January 30, 1999, 55–56).

13. An example of unfair competition as determined by the U.S. Tariff Commission is the dumping of steel on the U.S. market by Japanese, Russian,

and Brazilian manufacturers at less than the cost of production in producing counties.

14. By not very subtle inference, the target of the anti-welfare forces were black and Hispanic women; actually, the majority of welfare beneficiaries have been white women.

15. The lone exception is Switzerland.

16. A large proportion of violent crimes and much of the current pressure on prison facilities are drug related. Many observers, including this author, believe that the current very costly efforts to interdict the flow of drugs and to criminalize drug commerce and drug possession are bound to fail, just as Prohibition during the 1920s failed to reduce drunkenness while fostering organized crime on an unprecedented scale. The decriminalization of drug trading and drug use would eliminate the high risks and high profits in the drug industry and thus the criminal incentives, and enable government to shift its efforts to education and rehabilitation. Evidently, there is not yet sufficient public sentiment to enable any political party to support this reform.

17. On handling the problem of crime, the 1997 Gallup poll gave Clinton a 46–40 lead over the Republicans (*Scholarly Resources Inc., 1998*, 25).

18. While preaching the virtues of equal opportunity, Republicans advocate sharp reductions in and even the elimination of the inheritance tax.

19. The 1998 Mellon Foundation report authored by William G. Bowen and Derek Bok, presidents emeritus of Princeton and Harvard, respectively, demonstrates that affirmative action has provided the core of the emergent African-American middle class (*The Shape of the River: Long-Term Consequences of Considering Race in College and University Admissions* [Princeton, N.J.: Princeton University Press, 1998]).

20. The precipitous decline in admissions of Hispanics and African Americans to state universities and professional schools in Texas and California after preferential policies were eliminated in 1997 demonstrates the continuing need for affirmative action unless members of these substantial minorities are to be permanently relegated to inferior schools and excluded from professional roles in the American economy that require higher education.

21. On the handling of environmental problems, Clinton held a 53–38 lead over Republicans in the 1997 Gallup survey (*Scholarly Resources Inc., 1998*, 25).

22. 410 U.S. 113–1983.

23. U.S. Census Bureau, *Statistical Abstract, 1998*, 577.

24. The annual NEA appropriation of $120 million compares with the 1997 revenues of $22 billion for the Disney Corporation, a single source of popular culture.

25. In *Federalist* No. 23, Alexander Hamilton argued that an "energetic" government would be required to defend and promote the legitimate security and economic interests of the new nation.

26. American influence, however, remains limited by perceptions of national security and national interest among leaders of other states. Despite urgent en-

treaties, offers of economic incentives, and threats of economic sanctions, President Clinton was not able to prevent Pakistan from detonating nuclear tests in 1998, following India's example.

27. President Bush during the Persian Gulf crisis in 1990 and President Clinton during the Kosovo crisis in 1999 wisely exerted American power in the framework of international coalitions under the UN and NATO, respectively.

28. The Republican rationale for rejecting this treaty, that its terms were not enforceable, was vigorously contested by its supporters. On the enforceability of that treaty, see Hans A. Bethe, "A Treaty Betrayed," *New York Review of Books* 46; no. 18 (November 18, 1999): 6.

29. The IMF policy of requiring severe deflationary measures as a price for its assistance has come under attack, especially in relation to the economic crises in several Asian countries and in Russia. Similarly, the IMF's ideological commitment to the unrestrained international movement of short-term and speculative capital has failed to consider its effects on the economic stability of small and vulnerable economies. To the extent the United States finds such policies defective, it should use its powerful influence in the IMF to revise them and not, as congressional Republicans prefer, by denying the IMF needed funding.

30. Thomas L. Friedman, *New York Times Sunday Magazine,* March 29, 1999, 40–41. Friedman continues: "We have something tremendously special in America . . . but if we want to preserve it, we have to pay for it and nurture it. Yet when I listened to the infamous 1994 class of freshman Republicans I heard mean-spirited voices, voices for whom the American Government was some kind of evil enemy. I heard men and women who insisted that the market alone should rule. And I heard lawmakers who seemed to believe that America had no special responsibility for maintaining global institutions and stabilizing an international system that benefits us more than any other country." This is the essence of late twentieth-century Republican neo-isolationism.

31. *Statistical Abstract, 1997,* 182.

32. The U.S. contribution to non-military foreign assistance was 0.09 percent of GNP in 1997, compared to 0.45 for France, 0.28 for Germany, 0.22 for Japan, 0.81 for the Netherlands, and 0.75 for Sweden (James H. Michel, *Development Cooperation: Efforts and Policies of the Members of the Development Assistance Committee, 1998 Report* [Paris: Organization for Economic Cooperation and Development (OECD), 1999], 96).

CHAPTER 8

1. In 1996, 97 percent of black voters cast their ballots for Clinton, whereas only 48 percent of whites did likewise (Paul R. Abramson, *Change and Continuity in the 1996 Elections* [Washington, D.C., Congressional Quarterly, 1998]).

2. The gender gap, a national phenomenon, has resulted in a number of important Democratic victories in recent years. In 1996 women preferred Clinton over Dole by a margin of 54 to 38; men split nearly evenly. This is a critical asset for Democrats, since white males, especially in the South, continue to have a pronounced preference for Republicans. In the 1996 senatorial contests, for example, men in New York supported the Republican D'Amato by 1 percent, but women voted for the Democrat Schumer by a margin of 19 percent; in North Carolina, men supported the Republican incumbent by 12 percent, but women voted for the Democratic challenger by 19 percent, thus ensuring his victory; in California, men split evenly, but women voted for the Democrat, Boxer, by a margin of 18 percent. The March 1999 issue of *PS* includes several articles that speculate on the reasons for the gender gap.

3. In 1994, 34 percent of the voting-age population identified as Democrats, 31 percent as Republican, and 35 percent as Independent (U.S. Census Bureau, *Statistical Abstract, 1998, 295*).

4. The majority of seniors, having voted for Clinton in 1996, shifted to Republican congressional candidates in 1998, in apparent protest against Clinton's moral lapses.

5. President Clinton has appointed more African Americans to high office than any of his predecessors, cultivated the friendship of African-American leaders, and demonstrated genuine responsiveness to their concerns. This has not gone unnoticed by African-American voters, 97 percent of whom supported him in 1996.

6. In his 1998 re-election campaign, Democratic senator Russell Feingold of Wisconsin decided to limit his fund-raising and expenditures to $1 per registered voter. He refused to accept funds from political action committees or from sources outside his state. Though heavily outspent by his Republican opponent and with many fewer TV ads, he won handily by relying on an army of grassroots volunteers to spread his message by personal contacts and ringing doorbells. He also ran an active campaign on the World Wide Web. This pattern of low-cost grassroots mobilization may be exemplary for progressive candidates.

7. In the 1992 presidential election, whites with incomes above $90,000 voted at the rate of 90 percent; those with incomes under $15,000 turned out at 54 percent, and those from $15–20,000 at 64 percent. Minorities vote at even a lower rate (Paul R. Abramson, John H. Aldrich, and David Rohde, *Change and Continuity in the 1992 Election* [Washington, D.C.: Congressional Quarterly Press 1995], 109).

8. The Census Bureau estimates that 44.3 million Americans, or 16.3 percent of the population, were without health insurance in 1998—an increase of 833 thousand over the previous year (Reported in the *New York Times,* October 4, 1999, A1).

9. "Serving the Medically Underserved," *American Journal of Public Health,* 88, no. 3 (March 1998): 347–48.

10. *New York Times,* October 6, 1999, A20.

11. The unfortunate judicial decisions that exposed Clinton and future presidents to grand jury inquisitions organized by their political enemies and that required the president's closest advisers and Secret Service agents to testify against him under oath may have set dangerous precedents for the stability and effectiveness of the presidential institution. At a time when the burdens of future presidents are likely to be extremely heavy, these precedents may have highly mischievous consequences undermine the capacity of future presidents to govern effectively. This may be the most pernicious consequence of the rightist campaign to destroy Clinton's presidency. The cases referred to are *In Re Grand Jury Proceedings*, U.S. District Court, District of Columbia 1998WL 272884; *In Re Grand Jury Proceedings*, U.S. District Court, District of Columbia 5 F. Supp. 2d21; and *In Re: Sealed Case No. 98–3077*, 331 U.S. App. D.C. 385.

SELECTED BIBLIOGRAPHY

The Current Debate

Barber, Benjamin R. *Jihad v. MacWorld*. New York: Times Books, 1995.

Blumenthal, Sidney. *The Rise of the Counter-Establishment: From Conservative Ideology to Political Power*. New York: Times Books, 1986.

Carville, James. *We're Right, They're Wrong: A Handbook for Spirited Progressives*. New York: Random House, 1996.

Dionne, E. J., Jr. *Why Americans Hate Politics*. New York: Simon and Schuster, 1991.

Giddens, Anthony. *Beyond Left and Right: The Future of Radical Politics*. Oxford: Blackwell, 1994.

Grantham, Dewey W. *The South in Modern America*. New York: Harper Collins, 1994.

Gray, John. *Beyond the New Right: Markets, Government, and the Common Environment*. New York: Routledge, 1993.

Greenberg, Stanley B., and Theda Scocpol, eds. *The New Majority: Toward a Popular Progressive Politics*. New Haven: Yale University Press, 1997.

Hirschman, Albert. *The Rhetoric of Reaction*. Cambridge: Harvard University Press, 1991.

Hodgson, Godfrey. *The World Turned Right Side Up: A History of the Conservative Ascendency in America*. Boston: Houghton-Mifflin, 1996.

Kettl, Donald F. *Sharing Power: Public Governance and Private Markets*. Washington, D.C.: Brookings Institution, 1993.

Kuttner, Robert. *Everything for Sale: The Virtues and Limits of Markets*. New York: Knopf, 1996.

Lind, Michael. *The Next American Nation: The New Nationalism and the Fourth American Revolution*. New York: Free Press, 1995.

Lindblom, Charles E. *Politics and Markets: The World's Political and Economic Systems*. New York: Basic Books, 1977.

Lowi, Theodore J. *The End of the Republican Era.* Norman, Okla.: University of Oklahoma Press, 1996.

Nye, Joseph S., Philip Zelikow, and David C. King, eds. *Why People Don't Trust Government.* Cambridge: Harvard University Press, 1997.

Mann, Michael, ed. *The Rise and Decline of the Nation State.* Oxford: Basil Blackwell, 1990.

Steuerle, C. Eugene, Edward M. Gramlich, Hugh Heclo, and Demetra Smith Nightengale. *The Government We Deserve: Responsive Democracy and Changing Expectations.* Washington, D.C.: Urban Institute Press, 1998.

Stockman, David. *The Triumph of Politics.* New York: Harper and Row, 1986.

Strange, Susan. *The Retreat of the State: The Diffusion of Power in the World Economy.* Cambridge and New York: Cambridge University Press, 1996.

Weisberg, Jacob. *In Defense of Government: The Fall and Rise of Public Trust.* New York: Scribners, 1996.

Wishy, Bernard. *Good-bye, Machiavelli: Government and American Life.* Baton Rouge: Louisiana State University Press, 1995.

Yergin, Daniel, and Joseph Stanislaw. *The Commanding Heights: The Battle between Government and the Marketplace That Is Remaking the Modern World.* New York: Simon and Schuster, 1998.

IDEOLOGY

Appleby, Joyce. *Liberalism and Republicanism in the Historical Imagination.* Cambridge: Harvard University Press, 1992.

Bailyn, Bernard. *The Ideological Origins of the American Revolution.* Cambridge: Harvard University Press, 1967.

Barkun, Michael. *Religion and the Radical Right.* Chapel Hill: University of North Carolina Press, 1994.

Ceaser, James W. *Reconstructing America: The Symbol of America in Modern Thought.* New Haven: Yale University Press, 1997.

Commager, Henry Steele. *The American Mind.* New Haven: Yale University Press, 1950.

Galbraith, J. K. *American Capitalism: The Concept of Countervailing Power.* Boston: Houghton-Mifflin, 1952.

Gray, John. *Beyond the New Right: Markets, Government, and the Common Environment.* New York: Routledge, 1993.

Hayek, F. A. *The Road to Serfdom.* Chicago: University of Chicago Press, 1994.

Higgs, Robert. *Crisis and Leviathan: Critical Episodes in the Growth of American Government.* New York: Oxford University Press, 1987.

Nash, George H. *The Conservative Intellectual Movement in America since 1945.* New York: Basic Books, 1976.

Reichley, James A. *Conservatism in an Age of Change: The Nixon and Ford Adminis-trations.* Washington, D.C.: Brookings Institution, 1981.

Stourz, Gerald. *Alexander Hamilton and the Idea of Republican Government.* Stanford: Stanford University Press, 1970.

THE HISTORICAL EXPERIENCE

Appleby, Paul H. *Big Democracy.* New York: Knopf, 1945.

Banning, Lance. *The Sacred Fire of Liberty: James Madison and the Founding of the Fed-eral Republic.* Ithaca, N.Y.: Cornell University Press, 1995.

Bennett, Linda L. M., and Stephen Earl Bennett. *Living with Leviathan: Americans Coming to Terms with Big Government.* Lawrence, Kans.: University of Kansas Press, 1990.

Bensel, Richard. *Yankee Leviathan: The Origin of Central State Authority in America.* Cambridge and New York: Cambridge University Press, 1990.

Boorstin, Daniel J. *The Americans: The National Experience.* New York: Vintage Books, 1965.

Croly, Herbert. *The Promise of American Life.* New York: Macmillan, 1995.

Hofstadter, Richard. *The Age of Reform: From Bryan to FDR.* New York: Knopf, 1955.

Horowitz, Robert H., ed. *The Moral Foundations of the American Republic.* Char-lottesville: University of Virginia Press, 1979.

Kazin, Michael. *The Populist Persuasion: An American History.* New York: Basic Books, 1995.

McClosky, Herbert, and John Zoller. *The American Ethos: Public Attitudes toward Capitalism and Democracy.* Cambridge: Harvard University Press, 1984.

Miller, William. *A New History of the United States.* Rev. ed. New York: Dell, 1970.

Morison, Samuel Eliot. *The Oxford History of the American People.* New York: Ox-ford University Press, 1965.

Morone, James A. *The Democratic Wish: Popular Participation and the Limits of Amer-ican Government.* New York: Basic Books, 1990.

Reichley, James A. *Conservatism in an Age of Change: The Nixon and Ford Adminis-trations.* Washington, D.C.: Brookings Institution, 1981.

Scocpol, Theda, and John Ikenberry. "The Political Formation of the American Welfare State in Historical and Comparative Perspective." *Comparative Social Research* 6 (1983).

Skowronek, Stephen. *Building a New American State: The Expansion of National Ad-ministrative Capacities, 1877–1920.* Cambridge and New York: Cambridge Uni-versity Press, 1982.

Schlesinger, Arthur M., Jr. *The Cycles of American History.* Boston: Houghton-Mifflin, 1986.

Stourz, Gerald. *Alexander Hamilton and the Idea of Republican Government*. Stanford, Calif.: Stanford University Press, 1970.

Wilson, Woodrow. *Cabinet Government in the United States*. 1879. Stamford, Conn.: Overbrook Press, 1947.

_____. *Congressional Government: A Study in American Politics*. 1885. Boston: Houghton-Mifflin, 1900.

FEDERALISM AND STATES' RIGHTS

Allen, W. B., and Gordon Lloyd, ed. *The Essential Federalist*. Lanham, Md.: University Press of America, 1985.

Beck, James M. *The Vanishing Rights of the States*. New York: George H. Doran, 1926.

Beer, Samuel R. *To Make a Nation: The Rediscovery of American Federalism*. Cambridge: Harvard University Press, 1993.

Berns, Walter. *Taking the Constitution Seriously*. New York: Simon and Schuster, 1987.

Goldwin, Robert A., ed. *A Nation of States: Essays on the American Federal System*. Chicago: Rand-McNally, 1961.

Manley, John F., and Kenneth M. Dolbeare, eds. *The Case against the Constitution: From the Anti-Federalists to the Present*. Armonk, N.Y.: M. E. Sharpe, 1987.

Sundquist, James L. *Making Federalism Work*. Washington, D.C.: Brookings Institution, 1969.

Williamson, Richard S. *Reagan's Federalism: His Efforts to Decentralize Government*. Lanham, Md.: University Press of America, 1990.

CULTURE

Hunter, James Davison. *Before the Shooting Begins: Searching for Democracy in America's Culture War*. New York: Free Press, 1984.

Kelley, Robert. *The Cultural Pattern in American Politics: The First Century*. New York: Knopf, 1979.

Lasch, Christopher. *The True and Only Heaven: Progress and Its Critics*. New York: W. W. Norton, 1991.

McClosky, Herbert, and John Zoller. *The American Ethos: Public Attitudes toward Capitalism and Democracy*. Cambridge: Harvard University Press, 1984.

Rorty, Richard. *Achieving Our Country: Leftist Thought in Twentieth Century America*. Cambridge, Mass.: Harvard University Press, 1998.

Wills, Garry. *A Necessary Evil: A History of American Distrust of Government*. New York: Simon and Schuster, 1999.

INDEX